# The Afro-American Woman

# The Afro-American Woman
## Struggles and Images

Edited by
Sharon Harley
and
Rosalyn Terborg-Penn

Black Classic Press

# The Afro-American Woman

First Published 1978.
Published by Black Classic Press 1997
All Rights Reserved.

Library of Congress Card Catalog Number: 96–86019

ISBN 1–57478–026–3

Cover design by Oran Woolcock

Photos reprinted with permission from Moorland-Springarn Research Center, Smith College, the Schomburg Center for Research in Black Culture, the Association For The Study of Afro-American Life and History, and the Los Angeles Public Library.

*Printed on acid free paper to assure long life*

Founded in 1978, Black Classic Press specializes in bringing to light obscure and significant works by and about people of African descent. If our books are not available in your area, ask your local bookseller to order them. Our current list of titles can be obtained by writing:

Black Classic Press
c/o List
P.O. Box 13414
Baltimore, MD 21203

Visit us on the world-wide web at www.blackclassic.com

Distributed by Publishers Group West

*A Young Press With Some Very Old Ideas*

We dedicate this 1997 Edition to the memory of Dorothy Burnett Porter Wesley, Founder and Curator-Emerita of the Moorland-Spingarn Research Center, Howard University

# Introduction to the 1997 Edition

The seeds of this anthology were planted over twenty years ago when most of the contributors were graduate students. As African American scholars, we were concerned about the invisibility of Black women in feminist literature, which was exploding among academics in the early 1970s. The anthology was published in 1978, four years after the idea was conceived, only because we found it difficult to convince publishers that the book would sell. Nonetheless it did sell, becoming a classic—the first scholarly collection of essays about African American women's lives which placed us in an historical perspective.

The publication of *The Afro-American Woman: Struggles and Images* marked the beginning of a new field of intellectual scholarship—Black Women's History. Prior to its publication, studies addressing the historical experiences of African American women were few in number and generally not available in a singular text.

We focused on bringing the experiences of Black women to center stage, exploring our lives within the context of racism and sexism in American history and culture. For the most part, we took a Black nationalist feminist position, revealing how racism stood as the primary obstacle in the way of African American women's achievements. In addition, the contributors viewed Black women's lives and activities from a perspective inside the African American communities looking out, rather than as outsiders looking in.

Over time, Women's History developed in many stages, and Black Women's History became an accepted wing of the theoretical as well as the subject matter of the field. As feminist historians applied various theoretical constructs to the history of African American women, debates emerged during the mid 1980s about how we should proceed, as "class, race, and gender" became the catch-all phrase for most American social historians.

As feminist historians entered the 1990s, constructing gendered analyses of patriarchy began to replace thematic approaches in Women's History as the model for scholars, and historians of Black Women's History responded to the new directions in feminist theory. Some found venues for analysis which they altered to fit meanings uniquely applicable to African American women, while others resisted, arguing that our history had not been thoroughly investigated enough to abandon subject matter for theoretical analysis in the abstract. Still others debated whether patriarchy and/or class oppression were more significant than race as the major variable in determining Black women's experiences.

Aided by the plethora of scholarly publications in the field, many college campuses offer undergraduate and graduate courses in Black Women's History. Even with all of the new publications, there is still demand for *The Afro-American Woman: Struggles and Images*, which prompted us to reissue the anthology.

As we approach the end of the 20th century, however, one thing appears to be clear. Racism, though never absent, has reared its ugly head in much the way it did this time 100 years ago as Americans looked to the close of the 19th century. We cannot ignore racism in its new guise worldwide. As the "new world order," so designated by the leaders of the western nations, racism breeds the ideologies for scapegoating which find women of color particularly vulnerable. Consequently, reprinting this anthology, as we created it more than twenty years ago, is timely. It brings us full circle to view race as a significant characteristic of African American women's struggles and as a major defining factor of Black women's images.

—Sharon Harley & Rosalyn Terborg-Penn, 1997

# CONTENTS

**PART TWO: THREE ACTIVISTS IN FOCUS**

# DOROTHY PORTER

## FOREWORD

Since the feminist movement began in the late 1960s, resources for studies on Black women from their beginnings in this country to the present time have become more available. Holdings on women in various libraries and archives are being researched more than ever by students and scholars. While comprehensive bibliographies on Black women are lacking, more subject entries relating to them are being added to general card catalogs in libraries, and in some libraries special files devoted to women are being developed. Indexes to periodical literature direct readers to articles written by and about women. Some libraries, both public and university, have issued reading lists on women. Magazines like *Ebony, Black Scholar, Black World, Black Enterprise,* and others emphasize the important role of Black women in our society by devoting entire issues to them. Two periodicals, *Essence* and *Encore,* are edited by Black women.

An important exhibition of books, manuscripts, prints, photographs, and ephemera relating to women, 1500-1900, from materials in the Historical Society of Pennsylvania and the Library Company of Philadelphia was held in 1974, in Philadelphia. While there was little representation of Black women in the exhibition, the inclusion of Mary Still's *Appeal to the Females of the African Methodist Episcopal Church* (1857), in which she stated it was the "duty of women to carry the burden of enlightening Society," suggests the possibility of other items which might have been included. Exhibitions on Black women will give them greater visibility.

Within the collections of materials relating to the history of women housed at Radcliffe, Smith, Vassar, and Swarthmore colleges, there are to be found significant works on Black women. The Arthur and Elizabeth

Schlesinger Library at Radcliffe College, for example, contains the records of Pauli Murray, lawyer, educator, and author, beginning with her years at Howard University Law School. The Oral History project there has a taped interview with Dorothy Height, President of the National Council of Negro Women. A substantial collection on Marian Anderson is to be found at the Sophia Smith Collection at Smith College as well as documentation relating to the history of women, including materials on women's suffrage, slavery, works by Pauline Hopkins, and Black women's periodicals such as the *Women's Era,* edited by Josephine St. Pierre Ruffin.

Librarians of special collections in the major Black universities and colleges—Bennett College, at Greensboro, N. C., which has an Afro-American women's collection, Fisk University, Atlanta University, Howard University, and certainly the Schomburg collection in New York City—have regularly added subject entries on women to their card catalogs. In addition, they have exhibited works by Black women.

Fifty years ago, Monroe N. Work, in his *Bibliography of the Negro in Africa and America,* devoted chapter 30 to references on Negro women. It primarily included sources of information on Negro workers. Today, there is a need for a comprehensive bibliography on Black women—their accomplishments, problems, and status in American society.

The compilers of *The Afro-American Woman: Struggles and Images* have made a major contribution to our knowledge of little-known Afro-American women as personalities and the manner in which they have faced the realities of life, as they struggled for equality in this land, contributing more than their share to the development of American society. The biographical and historical research of the essayists has brought to light the accomplishments of Black women long neglected by writers in the area of Afro-American historical research.

This documented anthology about Black women is different from *The Black Woman,* a very fine anthology edited by Toni Cade, in which the Black woman of today speaks her mind. The compilers of *The Afro-American Woman: Struggles and Images* have presented to us, from an historical and a biographical perspective, Black women as civil rights activists, club organizers, reformers, abolitionists, lecturers, educators, writers, artists, composers, performing artists, and workers. We now have a more accurate image of the Afro-American woman and her place in history and in the cultural development of our society. This volume will stimulate research in a neglected field. It is to be hoped that the editors and writers will continue to research the lives and movements of Afro-American women of the past and present, so that young Black women today and those of future generations will have their heritage visibly inscribed in the annals of history.

# PREFACE

The history of the Afro-American woman and her role in the making of America has been neglected by historians, just as the history of women in the United States has been neglected. Much of the history has been of the black woman's struggle for equality in America. The struggle has been against sexism, which all women have experienced. It has been also against racism, which both black men and black women have experienced. This struggle has been compounded because at times white women created barriers to achieving the goal of equality for black women. Other times black men stood as obstacles to the development of their own women. For the most part, racism has been the greatest obstacle to the black woman's struggle. The essays in this anthology share several of the variations on this theme—the racial and sexual discrimination characterizing the historical plight of Afro-American women throughout the history of the United States.

The essays in Part One give a review of many historical experiences common to black women from the early nineteenth century to the 1970s. In "Northern Black Female Workers: Jacksonian Era," Sharon Harley reveals that any discussion of female factory workers in the North refers to white female workers, because black women were barred from factory employment despite the demand for factory laborers. Consequently, the Afro-American woman who succeeded as a wage earner outside of domestic service was an individual who forged her own success as a maverick. Although there were few choices open to black wage earners outside of service jobs, those available were usually reserved for black men. The struggle among black women for equality with other wage earners was twofold during this period, because it involved both racism and sexism.

Racism was not confined to the experiences of wage-earning black women. It was also experienced by black female reformers. The historiography about the woman's movement has been distorted to depict black women as indifferent or hostile to the feminist movement. In "Discrimination against Afro-American Women in the Woman's Movement, 1830-1920," Rosalyn Terborg-Penn asserts that black women were concerned about the same issues that white women campaigned against—slavery, liquor, and sex discrimination—but for the most part they were discouraged by white women from participating fully in the woman's movement. Prejudice and discrimination were elements that affected the daily lives of most blacks during the nineteenth and early twentieth centuries. Despite the rhetoric of equality among women in the woman's rights movement, black women like Ida B. Wells-Barnett and Mary Church Terrell were discriminated against in women's groups organized by whites. Although both women joined others who sought membership in totally black groups, they felt that black-white cooperation was essential to the success of the woman's movement. However, black feminists continually faced racism and sexism.

Basic to the struggles of the black woman was the way others viewed her and the way she viewed herself. According to Rosalyn Terborg-Penn's "Black Male Perspectives on the Nineteenth-Century Woman," some black men in nineteenth century America felt that black women were no different from themselves in that both were struggling to improve their lot in society. Because of their positive images of black women, these black men tended to support the woman's rights struggle. Other black men, showing paternalistic attitudes, viewed black women as being in need of their protection. Terborg-Penn reviews black male and female interaction during the nineteenth century, including the antebellum years and the post-Civil War period. In the latter period, black women mobilized against sexism and racism.

Cynthia Neverdon-Morton concentrates on the professional black woman in "The Black Woman's Struggle for Equality in the South, 1895-1925." Here again the question of white female discrimination against black women is raised. During the late nineteenth century, the woman's club movement became an important vehicle for reform among black and white women throughout the nation. This was also a period of severe racial polarization among blacks and whites, institutionalized by Jim Crow legislation and characterized by violence against blacks. The author examines the role of black female educators, who addressed themselves not only to issues like the need for kindergartens and recreation centers for black youths in the South, but also to the larger issues of discrimination, violence, and lynching, as well as the often unsuccessful attempts of black and white women during the early twentieth century to cooperate on common projects and concerns.

By the second decade of the twentieth century, the struggles of blacks in America, especially those of black women, were depicted in the songs of black female blues singers. The female artists described in Daphne Duval Harrison's "Black Women in the Blues Tradition" sang of their sorrowful personal lives and of the hardships facing blacks in general. The author notes that the woman's role in the blues tradition, as in so many other areas, has been traditionally ignored.

Although there seems to exist a limited view of the musical roles of black women, the myriad roles and images of black females have been portrayed in a number of poetic works. In an examination of poetic expressions about black women, "Images of Black Women in Afro-American Poetry," Andrea Benton Rushing describes the various images of black females that have emerged during the twentieth century. Although Rushing finds these images to be wider than those of black females depicted in visual media, she believes that the views portrayed still have failed to capture the essence of black women in the United States. She suggests several reasons for the incomplete picture of black women as reflected in the numerous poetic works she has reviewed. Although poets treat the image of black women as strong black mother figures differently, most poets tend to concentrate on this particular image. Other images emerge from the poetry, including the pleasing physical characteristics of Afro-American women, the positive role of black female singers, and, at times, the negative characteristics of the black female personality.

The essays in Part Two provide accounts of individual black women's experiences in the United States from the Civil War period to the 1950s. The experiences of Anna J. Cooper dramatize the double plight of black women who struggled against racism and sexism. Education was only one of the concerns of Anna Cooper, whose lifetime spanned over a century, from the mid-nineteenth century through the mid-twentieth century; in addition, she wrote extensively about the plight of black women in the United States. The personal crises and accomplishments of this Washington, D. C., educator are examined by Sharon Harley in "Anna J. Cooper: A Voice for Black Women." Cooper's reputation as a spokeswoman for black women reached national proportions, and she indicted black men for dragging their feet in assisting the women of the race in obtaining their rights. She fought the double standard established by the Washington school board for a "white" curriculum and an inferior "colored" curriculum. Shortly afterward, she lost her job as principal of the colored high school. Was she discharged primarily because of sexism or because of racism on the part of the administration, which could not tolerate a militant, outspoken black woman?

Another Washington black woman, Nannie Burroughs, was one of the few black women who successfully built and maintained a school for black women. Many blacks believed that vocational training for black women was one of the best strategies to obtain equality for blacks with whites. Evelyn Brooks Barnett describes the trials and tribulations as well as the political and social philosophies of this early twentieth-century District of Columbia leader in "Nannie Burroughs and the Education of Black Women." Burroughs acknowledged that domestic training was essential to black women, whose employment opportunities were limited by a racist and sexist society to domestic service. A militant supporter of woman's suffrage and woman's rights, she was hampered by black men, who resented her aggressiveness. The Nannie Burroughs story, like the Anna J. Cooper story, dramatizes the plight of a black woman who successfully struggled against the racism of the society at large and the sexism of black men—whom Burroughs and Cooper often indicted for their inability to give black women the support they needed.

Black women in the political arena have had to deal similarly with racism and sexism. Gerald R. Gill, in "'Win or Lose—We Win': The 1952 Vice-Presidential Campaign of Charlotta A. Bass," reveals the difficulties black women face in the political scene. Like most black women leaders, Charlotta Bass was forced to assume many roles in the black community. In addition to her political activities, Bass was involved in struggles for racial equality during her work as editor of a California newspaper. In no way members of the leisure class, black women like Charlotta Bass were forced to take on many roles which these essays attempt to capture.

# ACKNOWLEDGMENTS

Since the summer of 1974, numerous individuals have contributed to the success of this study. In the initial stages, we received advice, suggestions, and much moral support from Dr. Lorraine A. Williams, vice-president for academic affairs, Howard University, and from Dr. Okon Uya, now dean at the University of Nigeria at Calabar. As our project progressed, two individuals gave us their assistance reading manuscripts and making helpful suggestions. Special thanks go to Dr. Benjamin Quarles, retired distinguished professor of history at Morgan State University, and Dorothy Porter, director emerita, Moorland-Spingarn Research Center, Howard University.

On behalf of all the contributors, we want to express gratitude to the staffs of the various libraries and research centers who gave us assistance. Among these we wish to acknowledge the help of the staffs of the Moorland-Spingarn Research Center at Howard University, of the Schomburg Center for Research in Black Culture in New York, of the Library of Congress, and of the Trevor Arnett Library at Atlanta University.

In addition, we owe a special debt of gratitude to Dr. Arnold Taylor, professor of history, Howard University, for reading our manuscript thoroughly, and for giving us invaluable advice as well as moral support.

Most importantly, we would like to thank our families for their personal support of this and other scholarly endeavors over the years.

Sharon Harley
Rosalyn Terborg-Penn

# The Afro-American Woman

## CONTRIBUTORS

**Gerald R. Gill** is Associate Professor of History at Tuffs University.

**Sharon Harley** is Associate Professor of History and Chair of the Afro-American Studies Program at the University of Maryland College Park.

**Daphne Duval Harrison** is Professor of African American Studies and Director for the Center for Humanities at the University of Maryland Baltimore County.

**Evelyn Brooks Higginbotham** is Professor of Afro-American Studies and African American Religious History at Harvard University.

**Cynthia Neverdon-Morton** is Professor of History at Coppin State College.

**Andrea Benton Rushing** is Professor of English and Black Studies at Amherst College.

**Rosalyn Terborg-Penn** is Professor of History and Coordinator of the Graduate Programs in History at Morgan State University.

# PART ONE

## SELECTED HISTORICAL PERSPECTIVES

# SHARON HARLEY

# 1

## NORTHERN BLACK FEMALE WORKERS: JACKSONIAN ERA

The span of years from 1815 to 1848, loosely referred to as the Jacksonian era, has been described differently by various historians. Traditionally, it has been considered and even labeled by some historians, including Arthur M. Schlesinger, Jr., as the Age of Democracy or the Age of the Common Man. These labels supposedly apply to a period in American history in which the common man had an equal opportunity to participate in politics and an equal opportunity to advance economically and socially.

Not all historians consider this period an era of democracy—that is, an era of the common man whom Andrew Jackson symbolized. Such scholars as Edward Pessen and Bray Hammond believe that Jackson's common man was a small group of new entrepreneurs seeking to replace the old aristocracy. According to them and other historians, Jackson did not mean by "common man" the masses of people throughout the country.

The Jacksonian rhetoric of egalitarianism does not even appear to include white women or blacks, male and female. Women were considered to be inferior, socially and legally, and were called minors, if single, and if married, were under the control of their husbands. The concept of Jacksonian Democracy as it applies to one segment of the American work force, the black female wage earner, appears to be questionable. The purpose of this paper is to explore the view of Andrew Jackson as the champion of the working class as reflected in the work experience of free black female workers in the northern urban centers.

Although Americans boasted about their respectful treatment of their women, a few women protested about the way they were treated. Many women were afraid to walk the streets at night for fear of being physically attacked. Robert Riegel, author of *Young America,* reported that the explanation given for many attacks was that "the majority of sex attacks were made by a few degenerate males who could not distinguish in the dark a pure and chaste female from her erring sister."[1]

Many women enjoyed their inferior and dependent status in society, but there were some who found "the pedestal was an unsatisfactory substitute for their legal and social inferiority; by law, a husband had control of his wife's property, had exclusive use of her person, and could inflict 'moderate correction' by whipping or locking her up."[2] Women sought to uplift their own position through the formation of women's rights groups culminating in 1848 with the Seneca Falls convention, where the delegates issued a declaration calling for equality of the sexes.[3] Although the ideals expressed by the Jacksonians during this period did not apply to women, many women reformers based their calls for equality on these democratic ideals.

Probably the most influential and well-known feminists of the antebellum period were the Grimké sisters, Sarah and Angelina. The efforts of the nineteenth-century feminists were not very effective; nevertheless, the feminists formed a number of societies to aid their less fortunate sisters, such as the New York Female Reform Society headed by Lydia A. Finney.[4] The major focus of the women's rights movement tended to be on uplifting the status of the professional woman, not on relieving the plight of the more numerous industrial or domestic workers.

Ideally, women, whether black or white, did not work outside the home. Young girls assisted their mothers with the household duties until they married, and women with children were not supposed to work outside the home. But economic necessity dictated that some women seek employment outside the home, especially single women. In order to survive, a woman without a husband "took in sewing, opened a boardinghouse, did general housework, or became a prostitute."[5] Household work was considered demeaning to many white women, therefore the majority of household jobs were performed by black women, who had little or no choice of occupations. In the first half of the nineteenth century, factory work appeared extremely attractive as a source of income for those white women who did work.

The developing New England factories began to employ large numbers of women as well as children. The conspicuous absence of black female workers in the newly formed factories, many of which employed more females than males, reflected the racial animosity toward black females of both white employers and their workers. Although many northern whites condemned slavery, the majority were still hostile to free blacks.

MRS. FRANCES E. W. HARPER.

As a result, most women workers in the northern factories, like those in Lowell and Waltham, were white; black female workers were forced to concentrate their work efforts in domestic service.

At the beginning of the factory system in the United States, women began to dominate its labor force. In a report issued in 1816 by the U.S. Congressional Committee of Commerce and Manufacture, it was found that women numbered 66,000 while men only totaled 34,000 in the cotton industry, and the majority of the males were under seventeen. The 1820 Census of Manufactures in Massachusetts revealed that the Boston Manufacturing Company in Waltham employed 225 women and girls, but only 26 men and 13 boys.[6] Black women were not employed in factories in the northern urban centers until World War I, and not significantly until World War II. In the census reports of 1820, 1830, and 1840, information on the manufactures is limited, and the available information is not broken down by race. Since all blacks were despised and hated by whites, there can be little doubt that black females were excluded from the northern factory system, despite the fact that during the Jacksonian era, more women workers were needed than were available. Unlike black females, there were some black males who found employment in black-owned factories, like the sailmaking factory of black activist James Forten.[7] Black-owned businesses were rare and usually small.

Judging from the reaction of white female workers to the employment of the Irish in factories, one would need little imagination to predict how white women would have reacted to the employment of blacks. Frederick Douglass, black leader and editor of the *North Star,* reprinted an article in which the author describes why blacks were limited in their employment opportunities.

It is however, less the fault of the colored people, than that of the whites, that the variety of their employment is limited. The infernal prejudice cherished by our race against the African race has operated to exclude the latter almost wholly from what are deemed honorable employments.
. . . . . . . . . : . . . . . . . . . . . . . . . . . . . . . . . . . . . . . . . . . . . . . . . .
And of all Lowell's multitudinous factories, we presume there is not one in which the presence of a colored person would be tolerated even if he would work for nothing and board himself.[8]

Racial prejudice prevented blacks from working in northern factories as well as from playing a major role in the early antebellum labor movement. White women had no intention of working alongside black women; even if some of them did speak of sexual equality, most did not favor racial equality. Indeed, many northerners were hostile to free blacks and did not want to be in their presence at work, in their communities, or even in their churches.

Racial prejudice was so widespread that blacks were restricted mainly to low-paying, menial jobs. A foreign visitor, Edward Abdy, believing that there was not one trade in New York that employed black workers alongside whites, concluded that "the self-interest of the mechanics and journeymen is connected with the continuance of a prejudice, which thus shuts the door against so many competitors."[9] Fear of competing with blacks as well as the possible loss of job status associated with working with blacks caused white workers to oppose any efforts to have blacks as fellow workers.

Another foreign traveler, Harriet Martineau, wrote that the factories "afford a most welcome resource to some thousands of young women, unwilling to give themselves to domestic service."[10] Since household or domestic work was considered degrading by white women, these jobs were reserved for black females. A New York merchant who favored black women for domestic work asserted that black people were peculiarly suited to menial tasks.[11] The black female population was needed to fill jobs abandoned by whites seeking greater opportunities in the West or in the New England factories. White female workers more than their black counterparts scorned domestic work because of the low pay, hard work, and low prestige associated with this type of employment.

Although slavery had been abolished in the North by 1830, many racial motivations were used to justify the restriction of blacks to menial positions. Hosea Easton contended that whites had been instructed from childhood to "look upon a black man in no other light than a slave, and having associated with that idea the low calling of a slave, they can not look upon him in any other light."[12] Leon Litwack observes that whites, fortified with an elaborate set of racial beliefs,

argued that this situation indicated racial adjustment rather than economic exploitation. The Negro was simply unfit—physically and mentally—to perform skilled labor or enter the professions, he was naturally shifty and lazy, childlike and immature, untrustworthy, irresponsible, unable to handle complicated machines or run business establishments, and seriously lacking in initiative and ingenuity.[13]

In listing some of the economic disadvantages of slavery, John E. Cairnes quoted from a dialogue in Frederick L. Olmsted's *Cotton Kingdom* in which a slaveholder remarked, "You can make a nigger work but you can not make him think," to which Cairnes added, "He is therefore unsuited for all branches of industry which require the slightest care, forethought, or dexterity."[14]

This argument in conjunction with the racist stereotype of the immoral black female served to destroy any possible chances that Afro-American women had of being a part of the growing female factory labor supply. In order to alleviate any charges of immorality surrounding the factory system, many factory owners stipulated that job seekers "be of good moral character and industrious."[15] Factory owners stressed the importance of a positive moral image as a method of controlling the behavior of their employees. An observer of Lowell and other factories commented: "Of course, this control would be nothing among a generally corrupt and degraded class."[16] The significance attached to moral control automatically served to exclude Afro-American female workers, since the widespread sentiment among whites was that the entire black race was generally corrupt and degraded. According to feminist Sarah Grimké, the questionable morality of black women emanated from the sexual exploitation of slaves by white masters. Discounting the morality factor, Litwack maintains that "the same popular pressures that forced political parties to embrace the doctrine of white supremacy demanded and sanctioned the social and economic repression of the Negro population."[17]

In addition to the restrictions imposed against blacks' employment in factories, there are other possible reasons why black females were absent from factories. The possibility that working in one of the factories would increase a female's chance of getting married appeared to be one of the greatest inducements to many girls to leave home. Even if black women had had the opportunity to work in the factories, they would not have been attracted by the greater possibility of marriage proposals, since most black males thought the best place for their potential marriage partners was the home.[18] Another possible explanation for the lack of black factory workers during the antebellum period was expressed by the editor of the New York newspaper *The Rights of All*. Samuel Cornish warned blacks of the misery associated with factory work and urban areas in general. Cornish was not alone in his condemnation of factory work. The *Human Rights* and other newspapers reacted strongly to the conditions in the factories depicted by the female factory workers. In an article in *Human Rights* it was reported that "slavery in the South is heaven on earth, to the tyranny of the spindle of the North."[19] Wages were so low that in 1833 a New York doctor reported that there was a tendency for female needle workers to become prostitutes.[20]

Despite the failure of black women who desired factory work to obtain such employment, economic necessity dictated that most black women work. Unlike many white women, who were "supported, in idleness and extravagance, by the industry of their husbands, fathers, and brothers,"[21] many Afro-American women had to find employment in order to survive themselves or to help their families survive. Shut off from the factories, unskilled black females, especially in urban areas, were forced to work in domestic service at jobs which were more demanding than those most white female wage earners could imagine. A lack of available white workers native or foreign-born, enabled black women for a time to find jobs as maids, servants, and washerwomen. Oscar Handlin noted that most native white American women considered domestic work outside the home as degrading and added the remarks of the contemporary of the period who believed that most native Americans "would rather want for bread than serve to gain it."[22] Black females did not have the luxury of being able to choose which occupation they would pursue, because blacks were restricted from certain jobs. But free blacks still had to work:

> Despite these restrictions every state required free Negroes to work and their means of support had to be visible. As early as 1725 Pennsylvania had set the pattern by ordaining that "if any free Negroe, fit to work, shall neglect to do so and loiter and misspend his or her time . . . any two magistrates . . . are impowered and required to bind out to service, such negroe, from year to year, as to them may seem meet."[23]

In addition to being maids and servants, some black women held positions as "laundresses" and "seamstresses." Although their duties were similar to white factory laundresses and seamstresses, they were not allowed to work in factories, and their wages were considerably less than their white counterparts. Unlike the white female factory workers, who were usually unmarried, both married and single Afro-Americans washed clothes for a living. Racial prejudice against black male workers meant that many of them were unable to secure any employment. Under these circumstances, historians Lorenzo Greene and Carter G. Woodson claim, "the Negro washerwoman rose to prominence. She became in many instances the sole breadwinner of the family. . . . Without any doubt many a Negro family would have been reduced to utter destruction had it not been for the labor of the mother as a washerwoman."[24] Not all washerwomen were black, however, for some white women were forced to do piece work, for which they received 12½ cents for each shirt made, or 12½ cents for each dozen washed.[25]

By 1847, the majority of black Philadelphia women were washerwomen and domestic servants, numbering 2,085 of a total black female population of 4,249. In addition, there were 486 black needlewomen and 213 involved in some sort of trade.[26] These trades included dressmaking and hairdressing, jobs that were usually performed in the home. Although some black females as well as black males worked in the trades, "there was not a single trade in which Negroes were allowed to work beside white people. They were banished to the galleys of menial labor."[27]

Free black women, either because they were newly freed or because they lacked education or sufficient training, were usually unskilled; they were thus limited to menial tasks. In the city of Princeton, New Jersey, the only Afro-American female among the three most important free blacks was a domestic servant for a New Jersey college president. Education for black youth, male or female, was generally lacking in the northern states except where blacks established their own schools or where abolitionists set up schools for blacks. Despite the calls for improved educational opportunities for blacks by members of the Negro Convention Movement,[28] little improvement in the status of free blacks occurred.

As a result of the lack of training, many black women had to continue to perform jobs they had known as slaves: cooking, cleaning, and washing. In a survey conducted by the Pennsylvania Abolitionist Society in 1838, it was revealed that of a total 18,000 free blacks, 5,000 were live-in servants for white families. Not only did black women continue to work at similar jobs, the relationship between the free female wage earner and her employer tended to be similar to that of a female slave and her mistress, with some black females even referring to their employers as "mistresses."[29]

Before the Civil War, the free Negro in New Jersey enjoyed a status which was hardly better than that enjoyed by the freedmen under the Black Codes of the South.[30] Martin Delany asserted that southern blacks felt that opportunities as cooks, maids, and domestics available to northern blacks were really no different from the employment situation in the South. Southern blacks residing in the North were recognized as having said, "had they known for a moment before leaving, that such was to be the only position occupied here [the North], they would have remained where they were, and never left."[31] John Hope Franklin described an instance in which some free blacks from Louisiana became so disgruntled with life in New York City that they begged some visiting southerners to allow them to travel back to the South with them.[32] It is obvious that the lot of the overwhelming majority of free black workers was not in keeping with the democratic rhetoric of the Jacksonian era. But not all blacks fared poorly in the northern states; some black females were able to earn a decent living at respectable jobs.

In addition to domestic jobs, black women did various odd jobs, including selling flowers. One black female flower seller in the 1820s was a black woman named Chloe. In addition to selling flowers, she cleaned offices of the lawyers located near her flower stand. Besides selling flowers and cleaning hats, some black women had their own businesses, like Sarah Johnson, the owner of a hat-cleaning establishment.[33] There were a few black women like Elleanor Eldridge, who learned skills such as spinning and weaving. Although her mother had worked as a laundress,

Eldridge had a variety of work experiences, including working as a dairy-woman at age seventeen, which she admits was an unusual occupation for such a young black woman.[34] Another type of livelihood in which black women were engaged was hairdressing, as shown by an advertisement in the *Colored American* for "two small colored girls to learn the Hair-working Business in all its branches."[35]

In spite of racial prejudice and limited educational opportunities, some black women were able to enter professions. Sarah Mapps Douglass was not only a teacher, but also a writer and an activist in the Philadelphia Female Anti-Slavery Society. The first American woman to lecture publicly was a black woman, Maria Stewart, who was a public lecturer.[36] In addition to Stewart, Sarah Parker Remond and Frances Ellen Watkins Harper were lecturers for the antislavery movement. These women were usually looked upon with favor in the black community as examples of the accomplishments black women could make in society.

Afro-American male reaction to the working black female varied. Many felt that black females should not be working outside the home, especially if married and if economic necessity did not require them to do so. Martin R. Delany, a Pennsylvania black leader, did not object to black women who worked in order to survive, but was opposed to black women who worked when their husbands could provide for them. Giles B. Jackson and D. Webster Davis stated that "the race needs wives, who stay at home, being supported by their husbands, and then they can spend time in the training of their children."[37] Delany felt that the presence of black female domestic workers with working husbands was symbolic of the degradation of the black race. He wrote:

As an evidence of the deep degradation of our race, in the U.S. . . . there are those among us, . . . whose husbands are industrious, able and willing to support them, who voluntarily leave home and become chamber-maids, and stewardesses, . . . in all probability, to enable them to obtain more fine or costly articles of dress or furniture.[38]

In an effort to arouse the black man's opposition to such a deplorable situation, Delany exclaimed, "Until colored men, attain to a position, above permitting their mothers, sisters, wives, and daughters to do the drudgery of and menial offices of other men's wives and daughters, it is useless, it is nonsense . . . to talk about equality and elevation in society."[39] Like Delany, the black press extolled the position of black women as wives and mothers. The editors of the first Afro-American newspaper, *Freedom's Journal,* printed a declaration from another source stating that "the wife's occupation is to make her husband and herself some clothes . . . to washe and wryne."[40]

Although contributors to the black press as well as black leaders like

Delany felt that the ideal place for the married black woman was in the home, none was unaware that some black females had to work. Although critical of the female who worked just to be able to purchase luxuries, Delany had "nothing to say against those whom necessity compels to do these things, those who can do no better."[41] But those who did not have to work outside the home, in addition to taking care of their home and children, could "teach wage earning colored women the dignity of their calling and the need of making the race thoroughly proficient and reliable."[42] Believing that domestic employment should only be a temporary, stopgap measure, Delany maintained that for the black female "it has become so 'fashionable,' that it seems to have become second nature."[43]

For the majority of black female domestics, the attractiveness of such low-paying tasks held little importance. Recognizing the economic plight of the majority of black female workers, the black press attempted to assist them in obtaining employment by including in their newspapers such advertisements as:

WANTED: A first rate girl who can come well recommended to do the chamberwork of a small family.[44]

The editor of the *National Anti-Slavery Standard* included a plea for the employment of five newly freed Louisiana slaves ranging in age from twelve to thirty-one:

Places are wanted, in either town or country, for . . . colored women, lately slaves. . . . Wages are not so much a consideration, as procuring for them, immediately, homes in respectable families, where they may learn to gain a subsistence for themselves and their children.[45]

The editor of the *Northern Star and Freemen's Advocate* did his part in seeking to help black females find jobs. He included the following ad:

NOTICE: Colored Females supplied with situations in private families, or public houses, at Hutson's Office.

Good places and liberal wages warranted for good servants.

And in its very next issue, the editor printed:

The Public are respectfully informed, that those wishing servants, can be accommodated by applying at the office of this paper.[46]

These newspapers should not be accused of perpetuating the low economic status of black female workers; they were merely responding to the realities of life for free black women.

The editors of various black newspapers expressed their disapproval of the economic standing of the black community in numerous articles. Critical of the efforts of the abolitionist societies to improve the economic well-being of the race, the editors of the *Northern Star and Freemen's Advocate* stated:

For several years we have been astonished at the indifference manifested by the abolitionists in regard to the adoption of some effectual measures for advancing the welfare of free people of color. We supposed that while they advocated the rights of man and the cause of suffering humanity, that they would have been foremost in opening every avenue, and destroying every barrier in their power that was closed against us, or that retarded our progression; and that by doing so they would be able to present those with whom they plead for restoration of the inalienable rights of man, a class of individuals rising from degradation, and striving to become good, intelligent, economical and industrious citizens.[47]

Despite its efforts to help the female members of the race, the black press would not uphold the teachings of reformer Frances Wright as they applied to women's rights. In an article headed "Ladies Beware," the editor of the *Colored American* referred to Wright: "Male speculations and male achievements engrossed her soul.... She is now a leader in masculine infidelity—one of the grossest skeptical disorganizers that ever cursed the world."[48] Although Wright was condemned for her radical views about women's rights the black press praised her efforts to influence Southern slaveholders to free their slaves after they had repaid them in work output their purchase price plus interest. As an example to slaveowners, Wright bought and used some slaves on her farm in Nashoba, Tennessee, and set them free once they had repaid in labor what she had paid for them.[49]

Not all black women were able to find employment, even though many were willing to work at difficult and low-paying jobs. An article in the *Freedom's Journal* revealed that there were in New York City 43 colored women paupers and a larger number of white female paupers (462). By forming female benevolent societies, black women attempted to help their less fortunate sisters. The first such society in New York City was called the "Mother Society," which was devoted to charity and improving the lot of poor black people.[50]

Active opposition to their working conditions and low wages was limited for no other reason than the color of the female workers' skin. Black females had to be appreciative of what jobs they had and it was well known that the worst domestic jobs were relegated to them. With the increase in the Irish population, black women had difficulty even holding on to these positions. Their skin color shut them off from the antebellum labor movement. Supporters of the American Colonization Society pointed to the low economic status of blacks as evidence of their inability to adjust to American life.

The antebellum white women's rights movement did not speak to the needs of black women, and some women's rights leaders even ignored their poorer white sisters. Black women were not often welcomed as members in the white women's rights groups, as is clear from the antagonism toward the presence of Sojourner Truth and other black women who sought to become members of these groups. Northern white women were no less hostile to blacks than white males, as is shown by a newspaper account describing the stoning death of a Philadelphia black woman at the hands of three white women.[51]

Primarily because of the racial hostility of northern whites toward free blacks, occasionally leading to violent racial outbreaks in the 1830s, very few black women or men advanced economically as a result of Jacksonian Democracy. Throughout the antebellum period, black women were confined to the most tedious and degrading occupations. Racial animosity prevented joint efforts on behalf of the total working class, regardless of race, to improve the lot of workers. Since black employment was limited, black workers had to concern themselves more with finding employment and not the conditions under which they worked. Whites did not see the need for joint efforts with black workers in order to enhance the position of the working class. William Goodell attempted to point out the common plight of all laborers regardless of color: "A very great proportion of those who speak contemptuously of the capacities of the colored labourer, and doubt his capacity for self-government and self-control, are accustomed to cherish a similar contempt of all laboring people."[52] The failure of labor organizations to include the needs of the black worker in their goals was probably due to their fear that the inclusion of blacks would further weaken their already tenuous standing in antebellum American society.

Similarly, President Andrew Jackson and many of his followers praised the industrious, simple, hard-working man, but in no way included women or blacks in this rhetoric. In an era in which the common man was supposed to have greater opportunities to advance, free blacks suffered economically and socially under the burden of white racial hostility. Some historians have questioned whether Andrew Jackson spoke for any members of the working class, white or black, especially if they demanded improvements in their working conditions and life-styles. Lee Benson has observed that "far from championing or sympathizing with 'radical' working men, Jacksonian leaders denounced them for advocating doctrines that 'strike at the very root of established morals and good order of society.'"[53]

Factory owners did not recruit black females as workers, only whites, whose working conditions were ignored by the owners once employed. The depiction of Andrew Jackson as the spokesman of the working class was just as mythical as ideas about racial equality in the northern states. Black people, specifically Afro-American female workers, gained no significant benefits from the "rise of the common man." The egalitarian rhetoric of the period was never intended to apply to blacks, male or female, and as a consequence, Afro-American female workers labored under strenuous circumstances during the years from 1815 to 1848. This situation was true for the entire black working class. Northern whites, especially if they were followers of Andrew Jackson, were staunch enemies of free blacks "not out of rational economic fears but rather out of an irrational racism."[54]

# ROSALYN TERBORG-PENN

# 2

## DISCRIMINATION AGAINST AFRO-AMERICAN WOMEN IN THE WOMAN'S MOVEMENT, 1830-1920

Discrimination against Afro-American women reformers was the rule rather than the exception within the woman's rights movement from the 1830s to 1920. Although white feminists Susan B. Anthony, Lucy Stone, and some others encouraged black women to join the struggle against sexism during the nineteenth century, antebellum reformers who were involved with women's abolitionist groups as well as woman's rights organizations actively discriminated against blacks. The late-nineteenth-century woman's club movement and the woman suffrage movement of the early twentieth century were also characterized by discriminatory policies and contained individuals who discriminated against black women.[1]

The phenomenon of discrimination against blacks in reform movements is fairly well known in United States history. However, the prevailing historiography as well as the popular view of the feminist movements of the nineteenth and twentieth centuries is that white women welcomed black women into the cause.[2] Influenced by the rhetoric of female solidarity expressed by white feminists, recent histories of the woman's rights movement in the United States have concluded that because of disinterest, only a very few black women responded to the call.[3] When, however, one looks behind the rhetoric to examine the actual experiences of black women who attempted to join the organizations of white feminists, it becomes clear that the recent assumptions by historians need to be revised. In addition, when the neglected subject of black woman's rights organizations is studied, the need for further revision of the historical record becomes more apparent.

Not all Afro-American women sought to join racially integrated organizations. Some organized separate racial groups in response to common problems and to a common sense of identity. The trend became more pronounced during the late nineteenth century and the early twentieth century, when black men and black women organized self-help groups, which sought to combat racial discrimination and to express racial identity and solidarity on a national as well as on local levels.

The twin phenomena of antiblack discrimination in white women's organizations and the propensity of black women to form their own organizations raises several questions about the black female experience in the history of reform movements in the United States. Did most Afro-American women seek the security of their own organizations as a result of discrimination against them by white women, or did race consciousness stimulate the development of racially separate women's groups? Are there data sufficient to evaluate the role of black women in the woman's movement in historical materials left by white feminists and their organizations, or are there gaps in the data which have distorted the existing historical interpretations? A look at some of the incidents in which black women were either discriminated against directly by white contemporaries or discriminated against indirectly by historians who have neglected them in studies of the movement provides some clues to answers to these questions.

Discrimination against black women in abolitionist societies organized by white women appears ironic when one considers that white women complained of discrimination by men. Although some black women formed their own  societies or joined successfully with black men in such groups, others attempted to participate in racially integrated women's groups. The signers of the Female Anti-Slavery Society of Philadelphia, in 1833, included four Afro-American women: Sarah Mapps Douglass, the principal of the Institute for Colored Youth, and the three daughters of abolitionist James Forten, Sr.—Sarah, Margaretta, and Harriet, the wife of abolitionist and feminist supporter Robert Purvis. The same year, the Boston Female Anti-Slavery Society organized, with Susan Paul among the black members.

These Afro-American women attended the first two national female antislavery conventions, where the issue of receiving black delegates was raised. The first convention was held in New York in 1837, and there it was finally decided that "colored" members could be admitted. Sarah Douglass and Sarah Forten were among the delegates. Forten circulated her poem calling upon women to abandon their race prejudice and to join as "sisters" as well as Christians in their common cause. The body met again in Philadelphia in 1838, where once again the plea to abandon race

**Fannie Barrier Williams**

prejudice among white female reformers was heard from the delegates. Significantly, the same Afro-American women's names are listed in attendance at the national female antislavery conventions. Although the Forten sisters, Susan Paul, Sarah Douglass, and her mother Grace appear to have been outstanding leaders among female abolitionists, the paucity of black women in attendance is apparent despite the fact that several black female societies could be found throughout the North and West.[4]

Abhorrence of slavery was no guarantee that white reformers would accept the Afro-American on equal terms. In 1835, for example, Afro-American women began attending the Massachusetts Female Anti-Slavery Society at Fall River, causing such a controversy among the white members that dissolution of the group nearly resulted. Furthermore, Sarah Douglass, an active member of the Quakers, a group known for their participation in the antislavery cause, expressed her feeling of alienation from white church members because they discriminated against her. In 1837, she wrote fellow Quaker and feminist Sarah Grimké and explained how she and the other black members of the congregation were segregated from the white members on a special bench reserved for "people of color." Degree of skin color was also a factor in determining the acceptability of blacks by whites. Light-skinned Afro-American women appear to have been preferred in white female groups. Benjamin Quarles notes comments made to this effect by a member of the Boston Female Anti-Slavery Society about the fair-skinned Susan Paul.[5] Because of this antiblack prejudice, Afro-American women may have avoided participation in groups like the National Convention of Female Anti-Slavery Societies.

From the writings of the black antislavery advocates it appears, however, that white women accepted black men more readily than black women in their reform circles. Frederick Douglass, William C. Nell, and Charles Lenox Remond, all feminist supporters as well as abolitionists, have made note of the support they received from white female abolitionists. Historian Louis Filler notes that when black reformers turned to the woman's rights issue, few black women were prominent in the movement; the best known woman's rights advocates among blacks were men.[6] Among the Afro-American men active in the mid-nineteenth-century feminist movement were Frederick Douglass, Charles Remond, James Forten, Sr., James Forten, Jr., Robert Purvis, Charles Purvis, William Whipper, William J. Whipper, William C. Nell, James McCune Smith, Jermain Loguen, Henry Highland Garnet, and George T. Downing.

Historian Eleanor Flexner, a pioneer in the scholarly study of the woman's movement in the United States, acknowledges the work of black abolitionists Frances Ellen Watkins Harper, Sarah Remond, and

Sojourner Truth.[7] Although the names of Afro-American men more than double those of Afro-American women who have been noted as associated with woman's rights during the antebellum period, more black women were equally involved in the movement. Mary Ann Shadd Cary, Harriet Purvis, and Margaretta Forten participated also during the antebellum years. By the 1860s and the 1870s, Hattie Purvis, Josephine St. Pierre Ruffin, Caroline Remond Putnam, Louisa Rollin, Lottie Rollin, and K. Rollin were among the ranks of female suffragists. The names of these women can be found in the *History of Woman Suffrage.*

Sojourner Truth was one of the few black women noted by historians to have frequented woman's rights conventions. She, however, was not always welcomed. Her narrative reveals that the white women at the Akron, Ohio, Woman's Rights Convention in 1851 beseeched the chairman to forbid her to speak before the group. They felt she would ruin the movement by giving the public the impression that their cause was "mixed with abolition and niggers." In 1858, at an antislavery meeting in northern Indiana, members of the group demanded that she submit her breasts to inspection by the "ladies" present to prove that she was not a man in disguise. The "ladies" did not come to her defense, whereupon Sojourner rebuked them all and bared her breasts to the entire group.[8]

The alliance between abolitionists and feminists was further damaged during the post-Civil War years when male abolitionists argued that reformers should concentrate more upon gaining the franchise for black men first, then work toward female suffrage. Some of Frederick Douglass's strongest female supporters, like Susan B. Anthony and Elizabeth Cady Stanton, rebuked him because he failed to support their efforts to have the Fifteenth Amendment include women. Douglass argued in 1866, at the meeting of the American Equal Rights Association held at Albany, that the ballot was "desirable" for women, but "vital" for black men. At the meeting in New York held in 1868, Douglass reaffirmed his position in these emotional terms:

I have always championed woman's right to vote; but it will be seen that the present claim for the negro is one of the most "urgent" necessity. The assertion of the right of women to vote meets nothing but ridicule; there is no deep seated malignity in the hearts of the people against her; but name the right of the negro to vote, all hell is turned loose and the Ku-klux and Regulators hunt and slay the unoffending black man.[9]

Douglass's effort to keep the white women from abandoning the black suffrage issue failed. A majority of the feminists withdrew from the Equal Rights Association, whose chief aim was universal suffrage, and formed the National Woman Suffrage Association, which was entirely divorced from the black suffrage issue. Despite this rebuff, Douglass and other black feminists remained active in the woman's movement. Douglass reestablished his relationship with Stanton and Anthony immediately thereafter. On the other hand, white suffragists held Douglass's position against him and blacks in general as late as the woman's suffrage campaign of the twentieth century in spite of the fact that men like Robert Purvis had publicly renounced the Douglass position at the woman's rights meeting of 1870 in the District of Columbia. Furthermore, although Frances Harper had supported the Douglass position, she continued her participation in the suffrage movement and affiliated with the American Woman Suffrage Association.[10]

During the last quarter of the nineteenth century, the woman's club movement demonstrated, through the formation of woman's clubs on a national level, the desire of American women to assert their independence in the drive for reform. For the most part, these clubs developed along racially separate lines. Perhaps one reason for this development lay in the unique needs of black women during this period. White women had no need to vindicate their dignity in the midst of national cries that they were wanton, immoral, and socially inferior. White women did not have the severe problems of racial discrimination, which compounded the black woman's plight in employment and education. Moreover, race consciousness was evident among Afro-Americans in general as civil rights organizations, business groups, and self-help societies emerged with names signifying race.

Another reason, however, for the development of racially separate women's groups was the exclusion of black women from most white female clubs. Despite the differences between the two groups, there were some common causes and attempts at unity on local levels. Black women were involved in temperance work, suffrage groups, and club work. Nevertheless, the experiences of Frances Ellen Watkins Harper, Josephine St. Pierre Ruffin, Mary Church Terrell, and Ida B. Wells-Barnett indicate the pervasiveness of white female prejudice and discrimination against black females in woman's groups.

Afro-American participation in the temperance movement dated back to the 1830s. Roslyn Cleagle, in her study of the colored temperance movement from 1830 to 1860, concluded that black women joined with white women to form temperance groups because they were discriminated against by men and that blacks formed their own associations of men and women because they were discriminated against by whites. Despite Cleagle's assumption that black and white women worked together without discrimination prior to the Civil War, the experiences of black women in the antislavery organizations as well as the policies of the

Woman's Christian Temperance Union (WCTU) indicate that the opposite was true. Moreover, Cleagle neglects to explain why so many Afro-American women formed their own organizations if the New England Colored Temperance Society was the only men's club that discriminated against black women desiring membership. In addition, it should be noted that although white feminist Amelia Bloomer protested discriminatory policies against Afro-American men and women during the antebellum temperance movement, the policies of the WCTU, founded in 1874, encouraged separate black and white local unions.[11]

Frances Harper, the black pioneer in the WCTU, spoke highly of the movement, encouraging blacks to join the segregated local unions because she believed alcohol was one of the root causes of disruption among black families. Her reports during the late 1880s indicate, however, that prejudice was prevalent not only among southern locals, but among northern and western clubs as well. Convinced that temperance was essential to black people, Harper admitted that she was nevertheless reluctant to approach the local Philadelphia union although she had spoken on behalf of temperance many times in the past. With respect to the Philadelphia union, she noted:

For years I knew little of its proceedings, and was not sure that colored comradeship was very desirable, but having attended a local union in Philadelphia, I was asked to join and acceded to the request, and was made city and afterwards state superintendent of work among colored people. Since then, for several years I have held the position of the National Superintendent of work among the colored people of the north.[12]

When Harper was appointed to the national office, no other black women held positions on the executive committee or on the board of superintendents. However, the race question was an issue which concerned her because "some of the members of different unions have met the question in a liberal and Christian manner, others have not seemed ... to make the distinction between Christian affiliation and social equality." In 1889, Harper published a summary of reports from the black state superintendents throughout the nation. The attitudes which prevailed among black women reflected race identity on the one hand and the issue of discrimination against black women by white women on the other.[13]

Throughout the 1890s, Josephine St. Pierre Ruffin, a younger contemporary of Harper, challenged white women to unite with blacks for the benefit of humanity. Her words went unheeded. She was discriminated against personally when attending the Milwaukee convention of the General Federation of Women's Clubs in 1900. Very fair in color, Ruffin was mistaken for a white woman by the female delegates until they discovered that she was not only representing the predominantly white New England Federation of Woman's Clubs but also the black Woman's Era Club. Her credentials were discredited, and the women attempted to bar her from the convention. After much protest on her part, Ruffin was recognized as a delegate from the white group, while her credentials from the black group were rejected. Disillusioned by the incident, the Woman's Era Club made an official statement which included the view "that colored women should confine themselves to their clubs and the large field of work open to them there."[14]

At the same convention of the General Federation of Women's Clubs, Mary Church Terrell, president of the National Association of Colored Women, was refused permission to bring the group greetings on behalf of her association because the southern clubs objected, threatening resignation. Despite this rebuff, Mary Church Terrell was invited to speak before other white groups during the early years of the twentieth century. At the Minneapolis Convention of Women in 1900 she addressed the group not only about the needs of black women but also about the prejudice and lack of sympathy on the part of white women. She indicted them for not extending a helping hand to blacks whose aims were similar to their own. The same year Terrell made a similar speech at the National American Woman Suffrage Association meeting in Washington.[15]

Ida B. Wells-Barnett, another nationally known black club leader, noted the attempt of Fannie Barrier Williams, a black woman, to join the Chicago Woman's Club in 1894. The all-white group split over the controversy created by those who wanted a black member and those who did not. After fourteen months of controversy, Williams was admitted. At the turn of the century, Wells-Barnett noted that the issue was still significant in Illinois when the State Federation of Women's Clubs membership made it impossible for black clubs to become members. Nonetheless, black women's clubs were so numerous that by the second decade of the century a large federation of colored women's clubs was active in black communities throughout Illinois. In 1914, Wells-Barnett helped to organize the Alpha Suffrage Club of black women, who were influential later in electing black Congressman Oscar De Priest.[16]

The experiences of Harper, Ruffin, Terrell, Williams, and Wells-Barnett were not unique. Fannie Barrier Williams, chronicler of the club movement among Afro-American women, assessed the attitudes of both black and white women during the early twentieth century. Of the attitude of white women's clubs she said:

While many colored women in the Northern states have been welcomed as members to white women's clubs as individuals, the question of their admission in some instances has given rise to some of the fiercest controversy over the colored question that has been witnessed in this country for many years.[17]

As for the attitude of Afro-American women in the controversy, she said:

The colored women have kept themselves serene while this color-line controversy has been raging around them. They have taken a keen and intelligent interest in all that has been said for and against them, but through it all they have lost neither their patience nor their hope in the ultimate triumph of right principles.[18]

During this same period, the woman suffrage campaign gained momentum. As historian Aileen Kraditor has observed, white supremacy was an influential factor in the strategy of the suffragists as the need developed for southern support for a woman suffrage amendment. As early as the 1890s, Susan B. Anthony realized the potential to the woman suffrage cause in wooing southern white women. She chose expedience over loyalty and justice when she asked veteran feminist supporter Frederick Douglass not to attend the National American Woman Suffrage Association convention scheduled in Atlanta. Anthony explained to Ida B. Wells-Barnett that Douglass's presence on the stage with the honored guests would have offended the southern hosts. Wells-Barnett, however, admonished Anthony for giving in to racial prejudice despite the potential setbacks to the woman suffrage cause.[19]

During the National American Woman Suffrage Association (NAWSA) meeting of 1903 in New Orleans, the *Times Democrat* assailed the association because of its negative attitude on the question of black women and the suffrage for them. In a prepared statement signed by Susan B. Anthony, Carrie C. Catt, Anna Howard Shaw, Kate N. Gordon, Alice Stone Blackwell, Harriet Taylor Upton, Laura Clay, and Mary Coggeshall, the board of officers of the NAWSA endorsed the organization's states' rights position, which was tantamount to an endorsement of white supremacy in most states, particularly in the South. During the convention week, Susan B. Anthony visited the black Phillis Wheatley Club in New Orleans. In presenting flowers to Anthony on the occasion, Sylvamie Williams, president of the club, indicated that black women were painfully aware of their position among white suffragists. She compared black women to flowers "trodden under foot," stating: "When women like you, Miss Anthony, come to see us and speak to us it helps us believe in the Fatherhood of God and the brotherhood of Man, and at least for the time being in the sympathy of women."[20]

Although those national suffrage leaders who courted black support spoke in terms of equal suffrage among the races while in black circles, their public actions and statements to the mainstream society were often contradictory. Alice Paul, organizer of the suffrage parade in front of the White House in 1913, had professed her sympathy for black woman's suffrage. Before the parade, however, the leaders asked Ida B. Wells-Barnett, who was representing the Chicago suffrage club of black women, not to march with the white Chicago delegation. The rationale was fear of offending white southern women. In 1919, Mary Church Terrell confided her feelings about Alice Paul to Walter White of the NAACP. Both questioned Paul's loyalty to black women, concluding that if she and other white suffragist leaders could get the amendment through without enfranchising black women they would.[21]

Why this suspicion among black leaders on the eve of the passage of the Nineteenth Amendment? In the past, nearly all the major white suffrage leaders had compromised their support of black woman suffrage. Despite endorsement of black suffrage, Anna Howard Shaw had been accused of refusing to allow a black female delegate at the Louisville suffrage convention in 1911 to make an antidiscrimination resolution. As president of the NAWSA from 1910 to 1915, she avoided offending the states' rights position of the South, which rejected universal female suffrage because black women would be included.[22]

Aileen Kraditor observed the strength of the states' rights arguments among southern white suffragists when she contrasted the positions of Laura Clay of Kentucky and Kate Gordon of Louisiana. Kraditor noted their 1910 positions:

Kentucky, with a small Negro minority, could, according to Miss Clay, afford to give the Negro full security in his voting rights, provided women were enfranchised. Her views on the question of Negro suffrage were moderation itself contrasted to those of Miss Gordon, who lived in a state with a very large Negro population. To her, woman suffrage should, if possible, be accompanied by a "whites only" clause, and she showed considerable ingenuity in her endeavors to make such a clause constitutional.[23]

By 1919, however, Laura Clay had amended her position. She proposed, at the Jubilee convention of the NAWSA, "that certain sections be amended with particular reference to those parts that would permit the enfranchisement of Negro women in the South."[24]

Although southern white suffragists remained somewhat consistent in their position on race and suffrage, throughout the period, northern white suffragists continued to maintain ambivalent positions. Jeannette Rankin of Montana, the first female elected to the United States Congress, courted black support for the suffrage amendment among black women at Howard University, in May 1917. A few months later, in October 1917, she took the white side in a labor dispute among black and white women working at the Bureau of Engraving in the District of Columbia when the white women protested against working with blacks. As a result, in his column in the *New York Age,* suffrage supporter James Weldon Johnson questioned Rankin's loyalty to black women.[25]

Carrie Chapman Catt, president of the NAWSA in 1919, was supported by Ida Husted Harper, editor of the *History of Woman Suffrage,* when she discouraged the black Northeastern Federation of Women's Clubs representing nine states from applying for membership in the national suffrage body. Both women felt the black group would offend the white southern organizations and hamper passage of the amendment. Both Catt and Harper had argued in favor of black female suffrage in the past.[26]

Despite white resistance, most black leaders, both men and women, supported woman's suffrage because they hoped that black women could help uplift the standards of the race through exercising the franchise. The vote was believed to be the panacea to race problems. When white groups rejected black members, blacks formed their own groups as they had done in the cases of the abolitionist, temperance, and woman's club movements.

The failure of white female reformers to include the activities of black women in their records of the woman's movement has led some historians to assume that Afro-Americans did not participate or were merely objects of discrimination. Historian Louis Filler contends that the paucity of black women in the antebellum woman's movement was not because they were not welcomed by white reformers but was due to the fact that black women regarded the antislavery movement as the more urgent cause. Filler's position rests upon a shaky foundation, however, for historian Benjamin Quarles finds that the black female abolitionists believed in equal suffrage not only between the races but between the sexes. If Quarles is correct, one must find other reasons why black women did not join woman's rights groups.[27]

Eleanor Flexner's interpretation of the black female reformer and her relationship to feminism is similar to that of Louis Filler. She believes that black women considered antislavery work more imperative than woman's rights. To date, the role of the black female reformer during the antebellum period has not been examined thoroughly. For this reason, the Filler and Flexner conclusions appear to be premature. For example, Flexner mentions the abolitionist and journalist Mary Ann Shadd Cary, but neglects to include her among the black feminist supporters of the day. During the post-Civil War years, Cary lived in the District of Columbia, where she not only supported and attended woman's suffrage activities, but advocated women's cooperatives, women's newspapers, and temperance. Throughout the 1870s, she attended meetings of the National Woman Suffrage Association and, in 1878, she marked twenty years of service to the woman's rights cause.[28] Although Cary's reform activities extended from the 1850s until her death in 1893, she received little recognition by the contemporary leadership of the woman's movement during the nineteenth century and by historians of today.

The Cary case is not an isolated one. In 1870, several blacks in South Carolina organized the racially integrated South Carolina Woman's Rights Association under the auspices of the American Woman Suffrage Association. Among the Afro-American women were the wives of black congressmen Robert C. De Large and Alonzo Ransier. K. Rollin served as the secretary for the group, and her sister Lottie represented the body at the American Woman Suffrage Association convention held in New York City in 1872. Despite these activities, when the history of the woman's movement in South Carolina was written for the *History of Woman Suffrage* in 1900, Virginia D. Young, president of the South Carolina Woman Suffrage Association, dated the start of the movement as 1890, the year her organization was founded. No mention was made of the group founded twenty years earlier.[29]

Furthermore, in the *History of Woman Suffrage*, volume six, editor Ida Husted Harper included only passing reference to the role of black women in the movement from 1900 and 1920. The historical fallacy has been perpetuated by feminists in the 1960s and 1970s as well. In repeating what history has taught them, they have assumed that black women heretofore have been uninterested in woman's rights issues. In describing the current participation of black women in the feminist struggle as a recent development or in describing black women merely as objects of discrimination in the woman's movement or in neglecting the participation of black women entirely, these feminist writers grossly distort reality.[30]

The black feminist movement in the United States during the mid-1970s is a continuation of a trend that began over 150 years ago. Institutionalized discrimination against black women by white women has traditionally led to the development of racially separate groups that address themselves to race-determined problems as well as to the common plight of women in America. At the same time, Afro-American women, motivated by a sense of racial solidarity and a special identity arising out of the uniqueness of the black experience, have tended to identify in their own way with the larger social movements in American society.

# ROSALYN TERBORG-PENN

# 3

## BLACK MALE PERSPECTIVES ON THE
## NINETEENTH-CENTURY WOMAN

During the nineteenth century, black men viewed the "woman question" from several perspectives. The strategies they proposed, the speeches they delivered, and the articles they wrote reflected the varying images which they held of women during the century. For the most part, Afro-American men regarded the struggle for human rights, the black struggle in particular, as the most important social movement. Consequently, they tended to perceive the problems of black women primarily in terms of the struggle against racism rather than as a struggle against sexism. To some black men, however, legal and social discrimination against all women was a primary concern.

On the whole during the antebellum period, black male leaders were more sympathetic to woman's rights than white male leaders. One must remember that by 1840 over 90 percent of the free black male population of the North had either never had the right to vote or had been disfranchised in states where they had previously exercised that right. Although the Fifteenth Amendment enfranchised all black men in 1870, within a generation nearly all of them in the South had been disfranchised through amendments to state constitutions. Black men were therefore inclined to be sensitive to the demands of other groups similarly disfavored. In reacting to the "woman question" on the basis of their own images of women in general and black women in particular, some Afro-American men perceived women as being in need of male protection, while most perceived them as equal to men. Some sought to uplift the women of the race, while others included women and men in the uplift process. Some viewed black women as particularly vulnerable to attacks by white society,

**Robert Purvis**

while others viewed the problems of black women in a white-dominated society as quite similar to the problems of black men.

During the early nineteenth century, black organizations with both men and women in attendance were prevalent long before the "woman question" became prominent in white reform circles. Although some black male advocates of temperance, abolitionism, and moral reform resisted sharing equal status with black women, their antifemale prejudice was considerably milder than that of their white male counterparts. In fact, an examination of some of the predominantly black antislavery and reform societies during the antebellum period indicates that black male reformers usually included the rights of women within the struggle for human freedom. They empathized with the plight of women because much of the legal and political discrimination that black men suffered was shared by all women as well.[1]

One of the earliest Afro-American societies of men and women was the Union Society of Africans of Newport, Rhode Island. A self-help society, two of its goals were to work for the good of the race and for the abolition of slavery. In 1789, this organization listed Bess Browning and Rebecca Folger as members.[2]

In 1845, feminist supporter and abolitionist William C. Nell was among the men of the militant New England Freedom Association who shared leadership roles with black women. Three females were among the thirteen officers of this group, dedicated to assisting fugitive slaves.[3]

Afro-American men and women also joined together in the colored temperance movement during the thirty years prior to the Civil War. Both Afro-American men and women had found the doors of most white temperance societies closed to them. As a result, the numbers of black men and black women who cooperated together in racially separate organizations through the North was high.

Although black women were not always invited to participate fully in conventions and societies on an equal basis with black men, male resistance to such participation seemed short-lived and less hostile than white male opposition during the period. After 1848, Negro conventions generally seated women, although the men reluctantly shared decision making with them. For example, journalist and feminist Mary Ann Shadd was admitted to the Philadelphia Negro Convention in 1855 after a heated discussion in which she spoke in her own behalf. On the other hand, in 1859 the delegates to the New England Convention of Colored Citizens elected Ruth Remond and a Mrs. Lawton to the business committee. In addition, Ellen Sherman and Anne E. Gray were appointed to the finance committee.[4]

In contrast, during the 1840s and 1850s white males were more adamant in excluding white women from their reform societies. White males often criticized women when they attempted to speak publicly. Abolitionist and feminist supporter Samuel May recalled the prejudice among men against female orators like Lucretia Mott during the early years of the antislavery movement. Former slaveholders Sarah and Angelina Grimké were challenged by men who felt they were stepping out of the traditional female place in society when addressing mixed groups of men and women about the evils of slavery. Even the American Anti-Slavery Society split, in 1841, over the question of allowing women equal status with men in the society.[5]

When the woman's rights movement formally organized under the leadership of Lucretia Mott and Elizabeth Cady Stanton at Seneca Falls, New York, in 1848, white women were feeling the peak of frustration in their attempts to realize human freedom not only for slaves, but for themselves as well. Both Mott and Stanton had been barred from participation in the World Anti-Slavery Convention in 1840 after traveling to London for the meeting. By the time of the woman's rights convention of 1848, however, the barriers to cooperation between black men and black women in organizational life were breaking down. Most black women had not the sense of urgency or indignation which motivated white women to become feminists. In experiencing discrimination at the hands of white women, black women shared the status of second-class citizenship with black men. Conversely, the black male experience had given black men insight into the plight of women as an oppressed class in the United States. For example, in 1853, black abolitionist and temperance advocate James McCune Smith was not allowed to take his seat as a delegate to the World Temperance Convention held at New York. Although the credentials of delegate Antoinette Brown were accepted, the white male delegates refused to grant her request to address the body. Events like this convinced men like James McCune Smith to enter the woman's rights movement.[6]

Indicative of the views of black men toward women was their attitude toward education. Black men often viewed education as a means of bettering civilization in general and the race in particular. Many reformers viewed education especially as an imperative for women as well as for men. The right to seek a meaningful education without fear of discriminatory practices imposed by the society as a whole was an early problem faced by women. However, black women were faced with two problems—discrimination because of race as well as sex.

Abolitionist Nathaniel Paul of Albany, New York, protested against the violent treatment black women experienced at the hands of a white mob in Canterbury, Connecticut, during 1833 when a white Quaker opened her school to black girls.[7] Paul viewed black women as being in need of protection from a hostile environment. His was the traditional paternalistic view of men toward women—combined, however, with a sense of racial solidarity.

James Forten, Sr., the wealthy sailmaker of Philadelphia, headed a family of antebellum reformers which included his sons and his three daughters, all of whom were members of the national female antislavery movement. The Forten men believed in an egalitarian relationship between the sexes. Women as well as men were expected to gain meaningful education and to exercise their moral obligation to uplift the race and the society. Forten's son Robert sent his daughter Charlotte to Salem, Massachusetts, to be educated; under the Philadelphia school board policies she had been denied admission to the public schools. James Forten, Jr.'s, speech to the American Moral Reform Society in 1837 indicated his recognition of the literary talents of Afro-American women as well as their right to higher education. He denounced men who selfishly opposed extensive education for women.[8]

By the 1840s, men like Martin R. Delany and Frederick Douglass had also emphasized the importance of educating women in general and black women in particular. Delany and Douglass edited the *North Star* on the eve of the formation of the feminist movement; they were both active in the Negro convention movement as well as the antislavery movement. Delany, unlike Douglass, was a black nationalist who viewed the problems of Afro-American women in a white-dominated society as similar to those of Afro-American men. Douglass, on the other hand, was an integrationist, a master reformer concerned with temperance and peace as well as woman's rights. Although these men viewed the "woman question" from two different perspectives, they both perceived women as equal to men in the struggle.

Delany expressed his feeling about education and the black woman in his book *The Condition, Elevation, Emigration, and Destiny of the Colored People . . .* and in articles in the *North Star,* wherein he explained why blacks must abandon their attitudes toward the traditional role of women. He maintained that black women were the backbone of the race; they needed training to prepare themselves for life's emergencies as well as to pass on to their children the values which would uplift the race. Emphasizing the need for black men to encourage black women to seek skills, he opposed limiting the goals of Afro-American women to menial jobs as servants to whites. His pleas for adequate schools for black women and career goals above that of domestic predated the woman's rights movement.[9]

Douglass's sentiment about education for women can be found in the pages of the *North Star* and *Douglass' Paper*. In defense of white abolitionist Abby Kelly, he noted how intellectual females had been criticized and accused of not knowing household duties. Douglass justified the education and cultural development of women for the good of society as a whole and felt strongly that a woman "has a right to the same intellectual cultures as man; her sphere should be bound only by her power."[10]

The female reformer was viewed with respect and gratitude by black male reformers, who, for the most part, believed both men and women should share the duties of correcting societal ills. In a speech which he delivered before the Ladies Anti-Slavery Society of Philadelphia in 1836, James Forten, Jr., gave encouragement to both black and white women in their crusade despite the prejudice against them. Noting the indignities and insults women had incurred because of their stand against slavery, Forten condemned the attitudes of male abolitionists who felt a woman's place was in the home rather than in reform circles. Forten believed that public opinion, which at that time was white, male opinion, would favor eventually the right of women to become educated as well as to participate actively in reforming society.[11]

Robert Purvis, James Forten, Jr.'s brother-in-law, practiced his belief in woman's equality with man. His wife, Harriet Forten, was an active abolitionist and participated with him as a conductor on the Underground Railroad from their home in Byberry, Pennsylvania. In 1837, Robert Purvis joined with William Whipper of Pennsylvania in introducing the following resolution at the American Moral Reform Society meeting:

Resolved that these women who are now pleading the cause of humanity, and devoting their time, talents, and industry, to the cause of universal Freedom, deserve the blessings of Heaven and the gratitude of posterity.[12]

Some years later, in 1842, Purvis delivered a eulogy upon the death of his father-in-law, James Forten, Sr., wherein Purvis acknowledged the belief in the philosophy of the equality of men and women. He stated that "God has given both to man and woman the same intellectual capabilities and made them subject alike to the same moral government." Furthermore, throughout the 1850s, Purvis was a regular participant in the woman's rights movement. For several years from 1853 to 1860, he served as vice-president of the National Woman's Rights Convention, an organization of which his wife was also a member.[13]

Both Forten and Purvis participated actively with white abolitionists in Philadelphia. They seem to have viewed the discrimination against women as a universal problem rather than a race problem at this time. In contrast, white female abolitionists testified to the widespread belief among white men that women should not participate equally with them in the antislavery cause during the early 1840s. A significant test came in London at the World Anti-Slavery Convention of 1840. Several American women representing the American Anti-Slavery Society, among others, were sent as delegates. A large majority of the male delegates agreed with Nathaniel Colver, who charged that women were "constitutionally unfit for public or business meetings." As a consequence, the women were denied admittance to the convention as delegates, but were allowed to sit as observers.[14]

Charles Lenox Remond, perhaps the most renowned black orator of the day, arrived at the convention shortly after the controversy. He, along with William Lloyd Garrison, president of the American Anti-Slavery Society, and Nathaniel Roger, editor of the *Herald of Freedom,* refused to take their seats as delegates and joined the women as observers. Recording his feelings about the convention in a letter to editor Charles B. Ray, which was printed in the *Colored American* and reprinted in the *Liberator,* Remond acknowledged his indebtedness to the three female antislavery societies that had provided him financial support for his trip as well as moral support for the antislavery cause.[15] Remond's view of women was similar to that of Douglass, Forten, and Purvis. His family was actively involved in the abolitionist struggle. His sister Sarah and his sister-in-law Ruth were known in the movement.

William C. Nell also expressed gratitude for female support in the antislavery movement. An important Boston activist, he worked not only for the abolition of slavery but for equal school rights for black children with white children in Boston. In 1848, Nell addressed the Woman's Rights Convention at Rochester, New York, where he commended the energies and devotion of the women in the abolitionist struggle—who, he believed, were equal to men. Nell added that he would be grateful always to the female abolitionists for their work to set blacks free.[16]

The *North Star* editors seem to have supported women in the reform movement from the newspaper's beginning. Frederick Douglass admitted later, in his autobiography, that his main concern during the period had been the abolition of slavery; however, like many of his peers, he was grateful to women's groups and assisted them whenever he could. From March 24 to August 11, 1848, the *North Star* contained the "Address of the Anti-Slavery Women of Western New York," whose appeal was published weekly without interruption. Douglass also attended the Woman's Rights Convention at Rochester in the same year and reported the proceedings in the paper. Among several things, he detected male resistance among the whites at the meeting and noted the sexist statement of at least one, who thought a woman's place should be in the home rather than on a public platform. Douglass editorialized that black men should become more involved in the struggle for woman's rights because of their common plight. He also criticized the argument used by patronizing men who claimed that because women were inferior to men they needed male protection.[17]

Both Martin Delany and Frederick Douglass attended the National Convention of Colored Freemen held in Cleveland in 1848. Delany proposed the following resolution: "Whereas we fully believe in the equality of the sexes, therefore, resolved that we hereby invite females hereafter to take part in our deliberations."[18] In spite of the fact that the first woman's rights convention had been held only two months before, most of the black men found the acceptance of women in the political and business aspects of their organizations too radical. A debate followed, with a significant compromise suggested by Frederick Douglass. Since the convention had ruled that "all colored persons" could be delegates, he moved that the word "person" be understood to include "women." This compromise is important: although the conservative body of black men resisted political rights for women, they did not thoroughly oppose them. The episode was in keeping with the personalities of both men, Delany the militant, Douglass the politician.

Delany was able to realize his goal for full female participation in a black convention in 1854 at the National Emigration Convention in Cleveland. Twenty-nine fully accredited black women delegates, including Delany's wife, Catherine, attended the convention and, for the first time in a national convention, participated fully with black men.[19] Delany had firmly established the idea that black women were equal in status to black men.

Although Frederick Douglass opposed the emigrationist philosophy, he shared Delany's belief that women should share political rights equally with men. Of all the black male feminists of the antebellum period, he first publicly supported woman suffrage. He took his first stand in 1848 at the Convention on Woman's Rights held at Seneca Falls, New York. Douglass was the most prominent of the men and the only one to support Elizabeth Cady Stanton's resolution that women should have the right to vote. His eloquent remarks contributed to the successful passage of Stanton's suffrage motion. At the Woman's Rights Convention at Rochester, Douglass remarked: "In reference to the enfranchisement of women, it need not be questioned whether she would use that right or not; man should not withhold it from her."[20]

In 1853, Douglass was joined by Dr. James McCune Smith, an abolitionist and delegate from New York City, at the New York Statewide Woman's Rights Convention at Rochester, where black abolitionists Jermain W. Loguen and William J. Watkins were elected vice-president and secretary respectively. Woman suffrage was one of the major issues discussed and supported by the delegates.[21]

On the eve of the Civil War, Douglass continued his fight for political equality for women with men at the radical abolitionists' political convention at Worcester, Massachusetts, where he sat on the executive committee and invited women to participate in the proceedings.[22] The outbreak of the war in 1861 turned both male and female feminists to the Union effort. This signaled a break in the antebellum reform movement, characterized by strong white male resistance to women's aspirations to join in the struggle for human rights. The antebellum woman's rights activities among blacks, however, were included in the basic struggle for human freedom. By the end of the period, there appeared a growing egalitarian sentiment toward the role of women among black male abolitionists.

During the post–Civil War years, the old generation of black abolitionists continued to support woman's rights issues; however, a split occurred between feminists over the question whether women should wait until black men were enfranchised before pushing for a national amendment to include females. The Radical Republican efforts to gain the black vote did not include women; as a result, Republican politics strained the coalition between abolitionists and feminists.

Suffragists Elizabeth Cady Stanton and Susan B. Anthony had sought to connect the movement for black male suffrage to female suffrage as early as 1866 when the woman's rights convention in New York was turned into the American Equal Rights Association with universal suffrage as the aim. Charles Remond, George T. Downing, Robert Purvis, William Still, Charles B. Purvis, and Frederick Douglass were among the black men who participated in the interracial association of men and women. Douglass argued that the question of woman suffrage depended upon the preliminary success of "Negro suffrage." However, most female leaders disagreed and condemned the language of the Fifteenth Amendment as an affront to women because the word "male" was tied to the right of suffrage. Most, but not all, female suffragists abandoned the Equal Rights Association in 1869 to form the National Woman Suffrage Association, which was divorced from the black suffrage campaign. Douglass and other black men, among them Robert Purvis, Charles Purvis, and George T. Downing, remained active in the woman's movement; yet white female suffragists like Carrie Chapman Catt held the Douglass position against him, and blacks in general, even as late as the closing years of the woman's suffrage campaign of the twentieth century.[23]

The debate over tying woman suffrage to black suffrage was not limited to black men and white women. At the National Woman Suffrage Association meeting in Washington, D.C., in 1870, blacks disagreed among themselves over the priority for suffrage. Robert Purvis supported the woman suffrage position and demanded "for his daughter all he asked for his son or himself." Mary Ann Shadd Cary, feminist and Howard University law student, agreed with Purvis, as did Charles Remond and Sojourner Truth. Dr. Charles Purvis, the son of Robert Purvis and the first black surgeon-in-chief of Freedmen's Hospital in the District of Columbia, took the opposing view that had been expressed by Douglass. Poetess and abolitionist Frances Ellen Watkins Harper and George Downing also endorsed Douglass's view. While supporting woman suffrage, Harper indicated that if there had to be a choice between which came first, black male suffrage or woman suffrage, she felt compelled to support the men of the race.[24]

At the same meeting, white women attempted to discredit black men by accusing them of mistreating black women, an indictment which both Frederick Douglass and Frances Harper refuted. Douglass had not changed his view about the need for woman's rights and the ballot; he had simply reordered his priorities, identifying more with race issues than he had in the past. When he argued on behalf of the men of the race who were victims of violence and severe discriminatory practices, he was asked if black women did not face similar disabilities. Douglass argued that they did, not because they were women, but because they were black.[25]

After the passage of the Fifteenth Amendment in 1870, the antagonism between some female and male feminists intensified. James Sella Martin, black minister and editor of the *New Era,* in Washington D.C., noted that the growing antimale attitude among the women was injuring the cause of woman suffrage. However, within the year, Frederick Douglass was attending woman suffrage meetings and by 1878, Stanton and Anthony were reconciled with Douglass. He continued to be active in the woman's rights movement, attending nearly every annual convention of the National Woman Suffrage Association until his death in 1895. Susan B. Anthony was reconciled with not only Douglass but Charles Purvis, whom she visited in Washington during the 1890s.

During the last quarter of the nineteenth century, a new generation of black men, whose image of black women was in the tradition of Martin R. Delany, joined an increasing number of black women to identify the problems of the race and to seek the solutions to them. Afro-American women were victims of poverty and mistreatment, especially in the South. The northern press appeared to justify the slanderous attacks upon the morality of black women while they indicted black men for alleged violations upon "virtuous" white women. By the turn of the century, discrimination in the form of Jim Crow policies in all segments of public and organizational life were the rule throughout the nation.

At the beginning of this period, in the South, black men looked optimistically to the suffrage as a means of solving the problems of the race. As early as 1868, William J. Whipper, the son of feminist supporter William Whipper of Pennsylvania, had demanded that the South Carolina Constitutional Convention extend universal suffrage without regard to race or sex. Whipper had been a lawyer in Detroit and had settled in Beaufort, South Carolina, after the Civil War. He married Frances Rollin, the nineteenth-century biographer of Martin Delany; she, like her sisters Lottie, Louisa, and K., was an active feminist and politician. Whipper viewed women as equals of men and as citizens who should have a voice in government. Although his argument did not successfully convince the majority of the convention delegates to support woman suffrage, his family continued with him to urge female suffrage. His brother-in-law, Congressman Robert Brown Elliott, supported woman suffrage. In 1870, Lottie Rollin directed suffrage proceedings at the capitol in Columbia, where Whipper delivered a speech in favor of woman suffrage. She also represented the South Carolina Woman's Rights Association at the convention of the American Woman Suffrage Association in 1870 in New York City. This interracial group of men and women was organized by her sister, K. Rollin, in 1870. The leaders included the wives of black congressmen Robert De Large and Alonzo Ransier as well as William Whipper.[26]

In 1874, Alonzo Ransier represented this association at the convention of the National Woman Suffrage Association in Washington. That same year, he debated in Congress that equal political rights should be extended to all women: "And may the day be not far distant when American citizenship in civil and political rights and public privileges shall cover not only those of our sex, but those of the opposite one also."[27]

During the late 1870s, David Augustus Straker participated also in South Carolina politics. A classmate of black suffragists Mary Ann Shadd Cary and Charlotte Ray, Straker graduated from the Howard University Law School in 1870. In 1874 he delivered a speech supporting woman's suffrage at the Pioneer Lyceum in the District of Columbia. Many prominent black men attended the meeting and were impressed with his argument. Feminist supporters Robert Brown Elliott, Alexander Augusta, and George T. Downing were among those who persuaded Straker to publish his speech. Straker's image of women was similar to that of Whipper; he believed that suffrage was the right of all citizens, both males and females. In addition, he maintained that the same argument used against the enfranchisement of black men—inferiority—was being used against granting suffrage to women. Women, he argued, were no more inferior human beings than black men, and woman suffrage was not only lawful but was for the good of society. Former abolitionist and dean of the Howard University Law School John M. Langston responded favorably to the Straker address, stating, "I am myself, in favor of woman's voting."[28]

New York Republican State Committeeman-at-Large William Henry Johnson wrote an essay in 1894 which expressed sentiments similar to those of David Straker. Johnson attacked the traditional reasons men voiced in objection to woman suffrage. According to Johnson, women were as capable as men of making political decisions. He equated the prejudice against women to the same bigotry and ignorance that had supported slavery. Johnson went further, praising both black and white women who had fought for human rights. He included Lucretia Mott, Frances Harper, and Elizabeth Cady Stanton, all of whom were active in the woman suffrage movement. He felt that the time had come for men to abrogate their dictatorial political status and to share the franchise with women.[29]

The defeat of the Force Bill (1890) helped to dispel for black leaders the view of the suffrage as the panacea to race problems in America. Although many surviving black abolitionists, like Johnson, and the new generation of black leaders still believed in the right of women to the suffrage, the political future of blacks, both national and local, appeared bleak. Other proposals for solving the growing problems of blacks began to surface. Some Afro-American leaders began to stress economic security, if not political rights, for both the men and women of the race. The development of useful and practical skills was believed to be a means of eliminating poverty as well as a means of uplifting the race. In this respect, black men perceived black women equally with black men as victims of a racist society and in need of social uplift.

The Howard University Medical School faculty encouraged both men and women to enroll in the program. The class of 1869–70 had five women, and between 1870 and 1874 fourteen more had been enrolled; the first woman doctor was graduated in 1872. In an age when Victorian morality frowned upon coeducation, Howard University was not exempted from cries of discrimination from female students; but by 1873, the medical faculty had resolved to ensure equal treatment and facilities for female students. At that time, black feminist supporters Dr. Alexander Augusta and Dr. Charles Purvis were among the faculty. Both men held egalitarian attitudes toward women and sought to develop female professional capabilities twenty years prior to the emphasis upon skill development among black leadership in the 1890s.

The Reverend Alexander Crummell, pastor of Saint Luke's Protestant Episcopal Church in Washington, published his pamphlet *The Black Woman of the South* in 1881. He distinguished between middle-class "colored" women and "black" women. The majority of the latter lived in the South in what he described as a state of degradation and ignorance. Crummell rebelled against the acceptance of this condition by his race, and warned that if something was not done, the future of the race would be endangered. The development of industrial schools for black girls in the South was one solution Crummell proposed. Whereas Augusta and Purvis directed their energies toward educating middle-class women, Crummell was concerned with the plight of the poor, whom he viewed as vulnerable and in need of social uplift and assistance—from not only the men of the race, but from "colored" women as well.[30]

In 1893, two volumes dedicated to the accomplishments of black women were published, *Noted Negro Women,* edited by Monroe Majors, and *Women of Distinction,* edited by Lawson Scruggs. Both works were in the tradition of Martin R. Delany, William Wells Brown, and William C. Nell, all of whom had published books that included biographical sketches of Afro-American women during the antebellum period. Monroe Majors was born in Waco, Texas, and educated in Freedmen's Bureau schools. He graduated from Meharry Medical College in 1883 and founded the first black medical association in the United States. The title page of his collection carried the following mottos:

A race, no less than a nation, is prosperous in proportion to the intelligence of its women.

A criterion for Negro civilization is the intelligence, purity and high motives of its women.[31]

Lawson Scruggs was born a slave in Virginia on the eve of the Civil War. He was educated mainly through the efforts of the Baptist Home Mission Society and earned his medical degree from Shaw University in 1887. His collection was similar to that of Majors in that it dramatized the accomplishments of black women who had worked to uplift the race during the antebellum and post-Civil War years. Scruggs included an article by Josephine Turpin Washington that indicted blacks who fostered "the idea of the comparative unimportance of educating the women of the race." Calvin Chase, editor of the *Washington Bee,* praised Scruggs for his book, and Chase encouraged blacks to buy it.[32] Both Majors and Scruggs expanded their works to include the more fortunate female representatives of the race; however, the question of woman suffrage was never raised. Like Crummell, they sought to place black women on pedestals heretofore denied.

James T. Haley, the editor of the *Afro-American Encyclopaedia,* published in Nashville in 1895, included articles by Gertrude Mossell, Lillie Lovinggood, and Mary R. Phelps. These women encouraged black women to seek higher education or specific vocational training in order to help themselves as well as the race. Haley pointed to the accomplishments of black female journalists, who were producing eight newspapers throughout the nation in 1895. He also included an article encouraging women interested in journalism to learn it well, then to demand equal representation with men in the field.[33]

The editors of the *Atchison Blade,* Grant Brown, Nat T. Langston, and William Harris, published their Kansas weekly during the 1890s and appeared to perceive black women in the same manner that Haley did, as equal to men in uplifting themselves and the race. In 1892, they printed an appeal to black women to join the staff of the paper. Carrie Langston, from Lawrence, Kansas, wrote an article encouraging Afro-American women to better their lot, to seek educational and political opportunities, and to enter the profession of journalism.[34]

In addition to education, the abuse of black women by whites appears to have been a major concern among black men even before the 1890s. Alexander Crummell described the plight of black women who experienced sexual violation and "the loss of innocence" at an early age. In contrasting the black southern immigrant in the urban North with the white European immigrant, he argued that the white woman was allowed to be free once she came to America, but that the black woman was subjected to a degrading social life. According to Crummell's statistics from the 1880 census, over three million Afro-American females lived in the South. He predicted a bleak future for most of them unless a special effort was made for their social improvement. "Missions of sisterhood" was his solution to this problem. Crummell urged the educated woman of the race to teach less fortunate sisters domestic economy, cleanliness, thrift, and self-respect. Unfortunately, Crummell had no suggestion about how to prevent white men from abusing the women of the race.[35]

T. Thomas Fortune, the editor of the *New York Age,* was an active supporter of black feminists. He encouraged women to join the Afro-American National League, which he founded in 1890, and he attended meetings of the National Federation of Afro-American Women in 1895, speaking on the virtues of political equality. Fortune championed the plight of militant journalist Ida B. Wells (later Wells-Barnett) when, in

1892, she was forced by a white mob to abandon her press in Memphis because she condemned the lynching of three black men. Fortune hired her to write for the *Age* shortly thereafter. Fortune's images of black women appear to be determined by their circumstances. He viewed the independent, educated black woman as equal to the black men who struggle on behalf of the race. However, like Crummell, he sought protection for the vulnerable, poor, uneducated masses of black females, whom he viewed through paternalistic eyes. For example, Fortune complained that black women in the South were especially prey to sexual abuse and needed the same protection against it as white women. Although he did not advocate mixed marriage, he opposed the trend toward antimiscegenation laws in the North as well as in the South, which denied black women protection by law for themselves and their children of mixed blood.[36]

Fortune's attack upon antimiscegenation laws was in the tradition of earlier black male concern over the plight of black women. The report of the committee on grievances of the State Convention of Colored Men of Texas, in 1883, was presented to over 120 delegates with a resolution attacking the state's antimiscegenation law. The committee urged the convention delegates to petition the legislature to amend the law so that all "carnal intercourse" between the two races would be severely punished.[37]

Calvin Chase reported indignantly the assault of a Washington black woman by a white male. Because her word was questioned in court, Chase charged the judicial system with the use of a double standard for blacks and whites. A similar charge against a black man, he exclaimed, would have resulted in the man's lynching, just on the word of a white woman.[38]

Additional cries of outrage came from W. E. B. Du Bois, in 1899, when he agreed with a resolution made by the mostly male National Afro-American Council at its meeting in Chicago. The resolution condemned "the despoilers of homes and the degraders of womanhood." The young Du Bois had not yet made his reputation as an avid woman suffrage supporter; however, he was convinced that self-help and self-defense were the best solutions to the problems of the sexual abuse and the defamation of black women.[39]

Verbal insults waged upon black women were disturbing to black men, who felt that the prestige of the race was at stake. Lawson Scruggs expressed this view when he attacked the northern press for giving an erroneous view of black women in the South. T. Thomas Fortune also refuted the "wench" description of black women of the South. In addition, Monroe Majors talked of the virtue of black womanhood, which had been ignored by society as a whole. He hoped that his *Noted Negro*

*Women* would inspire young black women to look proudly upon the race.[40]

Racial unity was not only a means to enhance race pride, but the solution to the problem of white verbal and sexual attacks upon the women of the race. During the 1880s and the 1890s, the organization of self-help projects and associations was one segment of that solution. Du Bois was impressed with the women he heard speak at the meeting of the National Association of Colored Women in Chicago in 1899. He concluded that "thoughtful organization among Negroes shall enable them to act for themselves, rescuing and protecting their weak ones and guiding the strong."[41] An example of this was the activity of Alexander Crummell. He raised money for a home for "Colored Women" in Washington from the proceeds of the sale of over half a million copies of *Black Woman of the South.* Another example was the encouragement and support Victoria Earle Matthews received from T. Thomas Fortune in her efforts to found the White Rose Home for black girls in Harlem and in her work in the National Federation of Afro-American Women.

The other segment of the solution proposed to fight the problem of white attacks upon the women of the race was for black men to unite in defense of black women. In 1893, Fortune prevailed upon black men to discard their ill feelings about black women. He believed that the race could not succeed in overcoming the "taint" of slavery, nor build strong citizens, "until we have a race of women competent to do more than bear a brood of negative men."[42] The following year, Calvin Chase wrote a powerful editorial in the *Bee* entitled "Our Women," wherein he called upon black men to begin defending them as well as the race as a whole. He said, "Let us do our duty in defending our women; let us set up a system of reformation not only of our women but everything that pertains to the race's advancement."[43] Chase, like Fortune, was well aware that although some black men during the era had exhibited signs of male chauvinism, they could not afford to alienate the women of the race, whose social and political conditions were all too similar to their own.

At the turn of the century, black men continued to support woman's rights, and black women as well as black men united further in efforts to improve the lot of the race. By World War I, Du Bois, replacing Douglass as the most outspoken black male to speak on behalf of woman suffrage, A. Philip Randolph, and James Weldon Johnson in New York, William Pickens in Baltimore, Robert H. Terrell in the District of Columbia, Charles W. Chesnutt in Cleveland, and John Hope in Atlanta, championed the rights of women and woman suffrage. For the most part, men like these expressed an egalitarian view of the relationship between black men and black women.

# CYNTHIA NEVERDON-MORTON

# 4

## THE BLACK WOMAN'S STRUGGLE FOR
## EQUALITY IN THE SOUTH, 1895–1925

In spite of the fact that black women in the United States were not permitted to be fully participating members of American society, they were able to establish long-lasting educational and social service programs for poor and uneducated blacks. As individuals, in organizations which were exclusively black and dealt with black concerns, and in organized groups which professed integrative objectives, black women demonstrated that they had the motivation and skills to contribute to the improvement of the conditions of many within the black community.

Regardless of their contributions, black women were expected, however, to perform services which were considered "woman's work." Josephine Turpin Washington, a Richmond teacher and author, stated that many people believed that "the true woman takes her place by the side of man as his companion, his co-worker, his helpmate, his equal, but she never forgets that she is a woman and not a man."[1] This definition of the role of the black woman was shared in part, or totally, by a number of black men and women. Rosetta Douglass Sprague, the oldest child of Frederick Douglass, felt that educated black women could be most effective in the home. She saw their role as being the same as that of other women. In addition, she believed that black women could assist their towns in developing aid societies for the maintenance of kindergartens and industrial schools.[2] On the other hand, Rosa D. Bowser, founder of the Woman's League, a teacher for twenty-five years throughout the South, stated that the educated black woman had to be in front of the crusade against ignorance, vice, and crime. To do this, she had to go where the blacks were living. In further defining the relationship between men and women, Bowser stated: "Men are what the women make them.

Above all, the thought must be impressed indelibly upon the hearts and consciences of the youth that men can be no better than the women."[3]

Sarah Dudley Pettey, teacher and vice-principal in the Bern Grade School in New Bern, North Carolina, expressed similar sentiments when she asserted, "Men go from home into the world to execute what women have decreed."[4] In addition, she felt that only the educated, intelligent woman should head a household in order to insure that the young men would have received the best possible training at home. Pettey advocated that women initiate a movement to bring about compulsory education and general reform in the educational system of the South. The home training plus formalized education would help to establish for blacks a character of high morals, and high morals were necessary to combat the greatest white criticism of the race.

Mary Church Terrell, president of the National Association of Colored Women, suggested a new dimension to the role of black women when she stated that they must also be active in gaining social equality. This role was the most difficult one for the black woman to fill on a national level; consequently, very few black women, largely because of social dictates, participated in the struggle for educational advancement through decision making on either the local or national level. Terrell, an outstanding exception, served on the Board of Education in Washington for eleven years, beginning in 1895. In this role, she was called upon to make varied decisions concerning black youngsters in the schools of Washington. Her decisions were not always in accord with the rest of the board members. For example, a special meeting of the school board was called on May 26, 1910, to determine if a student, Isabel I. Wall, was white or black. The board decided that she was black. Terrell wrote a dissenting opinion protesting the decision and the board's determination that the child must attend a school for blacks. Having known the child's mother, she believed the student to be more white than black.[5]

Women in other parts of the South were also actively engaged, as was Terrell, in improving the educational facilities for black youth. Atlanta was the site of constant agitation by black women. Realizing that city and state governments were not willing to heed the advice and honor the petitions of black people if their goals were counter to the desires of whites, educated black women throughout the South felt compelled to perform a number of social services for the masses.

On July 8, 1908, Cynthia Lugenia Burns Hope, wife of John Hope, the president of Morehouse College, called a meeting of her neighbors to discuss ways and means of making practical the immortal command "love thy neighbor as thyself." Lugenia Hope was born in St. Louis but was taken to Chicago by her mother after her father's death. After her marriage in 1897, she made Atlanta her home.[6]

A result of the meeting called by Hope was the formation of the Neighborhood Union, wherein the city of Atlanta was divided into zones with each supervised by a chairwoman. The zones were then divided into districts. The districts operated under presiding officers and corps of workers selected from the neighborhood. Through this process, all efforts of the union would have the support of community workers and not just the efforts of educated black females. The union had two major functions relating to education. They were:

1. To provide playgrounds, clubs, good literature, and neighborhood centers for the moral, physical, and intellectual development of the young.

2. To establish lecture courses, classes, and clubs for adults for the purpose of encouraging habits of cleanliness and industry, promoting child welfare, and of bringing about culture and efficiency in general home-making.[7]

In 1911, the Neighborhood Union was incorporated. One of its earliest acts was to request the use of the schools for blacks so that vacation schools could be operated from July 6 through August 14, 1912. The request was honored. Local papers supported the efforts of the union and were thus able to elicit support for it. Classes were organized in serving, cooking, home nursing, and handicrafts, and these classes were held in the homes of members. To spread the work among many and to alleviate problems connected with meeting in neighbors' homes, a Neighborhood House was established, and in 1914 a residential worker was hired for the new house. In 1916 the Woman's Baptist Home Mission Society began to send $40 per month to Hope for temporary workers for the Neighborhood House. In 1924, the city of Atlanta gave $5,500 to aid the Neighborhood Union and recognized the union as a member of the Atlanta Community Chest.[8]

To involve other members of the educated populace of Atlanta, Lugenia Hope enlisted the cooperation of the students from Morehouse College, Spelman College, and Atlanta University. She organized a Social Service Institute on the Morehouse campus from September 23 to 26, 1919, in order to provide technical information to the students and workers and to supplement their skills. The Neighborhood Union's efforts were so successful that other cities began to request information so that it could be used as a model to fit their needs. Black women in Alabama, Virginia, and Tennessee adopted the idea. Mrs. William T. B. Williams, wife of the Slater Fund field agent, suggested that an article be written for the *Southern Workman* in order that blacks throughout the South could benefit from the experiences of the women in Atlanta.[9]

Blacks responded to the activities of the Neighborhood Union and gave meaning to the motto "love thy neighbor as thyself." In 1925, a West Side House was established in Atlanta. Two hundred and fifty children were attending classes in sewing, cooking, and flower making, and adult classes were being formed.[10] The Neighborhood Union was a success, celebrating its twenty-fifth anniversary in 1933.

The Neighborhood Union was not hesitant in requesting educational facilities and benefits for blacks from local authorities. In 1913, the women petitioned the Atlanta Board of Education for two more schools for blacks. The South Atlanta School had only grades one through four, and other schools which were established were grossly inadequate. On August 19, 1913, Hope, on behalf of the Women's Civic and Social Improvement Committee, again requested that the board of education provide better facilities for the children. The problems pinpointed were the need for toilets, special facilities for the retarded, and the abolition of double school sessions.[11]

Initially, the Women's Civic and Social Improvement Committee was organized under the auspices of the Neighborhood Union to work for better conditions in the black public schools of Atlanta. The committee met every week for six months and investigated every black school in Atlanta. The Subcommittee of Investigation of the Schools noted that the schools were very unhealthful; the light and ventilation were poor; the schools were congested; and the children were forced to attend double sessions. In seeking to change the existing conditions, the women visited white women to solicit support for the blacks' endeavors and also interviewed members of the city council and white pastors. Mass meetings were held and placards posted to make the general public aware of their concerns and efforts. For the school year 1913-14, the seating capacity in the black schools was 4,102 and the enrollment was 6,163. Two thousand and sixty-one pupils were affected by the double schedule. Both sessions had the same teachers. As a result of the work of the committee, teachers' salaries were raised; a makeshift school was established in South Atlanta; and black men decided to join the efforts of the women.[12]

However, efforts to improve the educational facilities for blacks in Atlanta did not cease when some success seemed apparent. On December 3, 1913, in an open letter to the editor of the *Constitution,* the Women's Social Improvement Committee advised the school board not to eliminate, as it planned, grades seven and eight. Atlanta wanted to limit the school curriculum to a literary course, which was the equivalent of six grades. In 1913, white children attended eight grades and had the option of attending a high school. The women's group desired that academic and industrial training be made available to black youths. They cited the school systems in Nashville and Memphis as evidence of the

**Charlotte Hawkins Brown**

effectiveness of a dual program. The women were not hesitant in pointing out that the schools were supported by all taxpayers.[13] The board chose not to respond to the open letters, but one of the purposes of the letters was accomplished because the citizens of Atlanta were made aware of the fact that some black women would speak out against inequities in the educational system.

In a direct confrontation, a group of black women of Atlanta went to the city council to protest a bill which had been passed on July 14, 1915. The new law stated that whites were not to teach blacks or blacks to teach whites. It must be noted that there had been widespread agitation throughout the United States among blacks to have only black teachers in black schools. The Atlanta women, even though they supported the principle of black teachers for black children, acknowledged certain basic realities. The law presented a serious problem because not only was it difficult to obtain qualified black teachers, but whites were currently on the faculties of the local black colleges and in the black public schools. If the whites were to be forced from the classrooms, a critical lack of teachers would occur which would curtail the education for many blacks. The women protested the act on the basis that it was unconstitutional and contrary to southern policy which had permitted blacks to be taught by whites.[14] Refusal to obey and agitation from whites and blacks caused the city to modify its position.

Not all efforts of the Neighborhood Union and the Women's Civic and Social Improvement Committee were successful. The greatest problems and failures occurred when the women challenged whites to provide educational improvements. The two organizations did prove, however, that blacks could work well together to achieve certain goals and did not have to remove themselves from direct contact with the masses. In time, the women of these organizations were able to turn over their responsibilities to paid workers so that they could be free to address themselves to other concerns. Founders of the Neighborhood Union and the Women's Civic and Social Improvement Committee continued to assist the organizations through the training of young black men and women in the field of social work.

Educated black women also addressed themselves to the needs of the very young. They believed that unless youths received the proper guidance at an early stage in their lives, they would be lost in terms of self and societal productivity. W. E. B. Du Bois spoke in the chapel at Atlanta University during the annual Atlanta University Conference (1915); his topic was "The Welfare of the Negro Child." Gertrude Ware, the Kindergarten Training School teacher at Atlanta University, led the discussion concerning the care of children left unattended while the mothers work. A few black mothers were in attendance at the conference. They elected to establish free kindergartens in scattered parts of the city so that working mothers would have a safe place to leave their preschool children. Du Bois asked Ware to organize the women to accomplish their goals.[15]

The kindergartens, located in slum areas, grew from one to five in three years. There was an average daily attendance of thirty children. The Gate City Kindergarten Association had twenty members, but only twelve were continually active. Concerts, fairs, track meets, contests, and other activities were held to raise funds. By 1925, the association had raised and used over $30,000. Alonzo F. Herndon, a black millionaire of Atlanta, gave a building for a nursery valued at $10,000, two gallons of milk a day for many years, and paid the salary, $480 per year, of the matron for several years. The first nursery was established in the fall of 1918. By 1925, there was a day nursery in west and east Atlanta supported by the Community Chest. Children over six were sent to the nearest public school. At the kindergarten there was a study period during which the youngsters prepared their lessons for school under the supervision of the matron. The kindergartens did not attempt to take the place of the public schools but were designed to supplement the learning and skills developed in the schools. In twelve years the association worked with 3,000 children and provided nutritious lunches and clothing for all the children.[16]

Lugenia Hope, filling many roles, served as president of the Gate City Kindergarten Association for three years. During subsequent years, Jennie White served as president. A public school teacher for thirty-six years, White also supervised one of the day nurseries. As a result of her success, the city of Augusta, Georgia, had made an exception to its rule that married teachers were ineligible to teach in public schools, thus permitting White to work. She also served as assistant principal and, later, as principal.[17]

Similar day care centers were established throughout the South. The kindergartens in Atlanta, however, were not the first. The Woman's League of Washington, D.C., was organized in 1892 and by 1898 had established seven kindergartens serving over a hundred children.[18] The women of Atlanta and other southern cities had demonstrated again that blacks could and would be responsible for one another's welfare. No reports of internal conflicts appear. The nurseries and kindergartens, demonstrating that the black community could provide black youths with physical comforts as well as early development of educational skills, continued after 1925.

Black women realized that in order for them to be truly effective in helping youths to develop, they had to confront some basic problems of women. To respond to their common problems, black women became active in the club movement. Fannie Barrier Williams, woman's activist, stated: "The club movement among the colored women has grown out of the organized anxiety of women who have only recently become intelligent enough to recognize their own social condition and strong enough to initiate and apply the forces of reform."[19] Clubs were organized primarily in urban centers, where it was easier for women to assemble for meetings.

In Hampton, Virginia, the women organized a club with several departments, the Home Maker's Club. All units of the club worked for some phase of home improvement. There were times, however, when common problems were discussed.[20] Some clubs reached out to serve the community. In 1897, the Woman's League of Lynchburg, Virginia, established a night school for those who were forced to work during the day. The regular day school teachers also taught at night. Compensation for the long work day was the knowledge that blacks were being educated.

In Montgomery, Alabama, the Sojourner Truth Club was organized by a group of women who eventually established a free reading room and library. In Richmond, the Council of Colored Women, under the presidency of Maggie Lena Walker, raised funds for black causes. They assisted in the development and maintenance of the Girls' Industrial School at Peaks, Virginia, the Community House in Richmond (patterned after the Neighborhood House in Atlanta), and they supported a black visiting nurse in Richmond.[21]

The women were also concerned with enriching their formal educational training. Throughout the South, women, white and black, organized literary clubs. The model most often used was the Chautauqua Assembly, established in 1874 by an Ohio businessman, Lewis Miller, and a Methodist bishop, John H. Vincent. The original purpose of the assembly was to train Sunday school teachers during the summer months. In a short time, the Chautauqua Literary and Scientific Reading Circle became a national society with study circles and nationally known lecturers, including several presidents of the United States.

The Chautauqua movement influenced five women of Atlanta, Marie Antoinette Johnson, V. Nora Bell, Mrs. Walter Covington (first name unavailable), C. C. Carter, and J. R. Porter to organize a literary group for black women. On September 8, 1913, a permanent organization was established at the home of Celestine Slater with a membership quota of fifteen women. Topics dealing with or related to women were selected for the discussions held at each meeting. Each woman researched her topic before delivery and was expected to be able to answer all questions about the topic which were raised by the other members. The circle also sponsored debates, lectures, readings, and social entertainments. The ladies, in an attempt to help those who were less fortunate, gave funds to organizations which were established in the interest of children.[22]

Black women also participated in organizations which were originally formed to provide services for whites. To help develop young white women along Christian lines, the Young Women's Christian Association was formed. In 1915, there were seventeen chapters of the YWCA for black women. Six chapters were affiliated with the national association but did not have enough members to warrant the establishment of local branches. In two cities women had established provisional chapters and had submitted applications for membership for twenty-seven communities. Prior to the establishment of the first chapter for blacks, Eva Bowles served as the secretary for "colored work" from the New York headquarters.[23] As did the black chapters of the YMCA, branches of the YWCA for blacks utilized in their early development black college facilities.

The central YWCA was not willing to allow black women to work independently in the branches established for them. When a branch was established, the New York headquarters enumerated specific guidelines it had to follow. A committee of affiliation had to be appointed, which included three or five white women and three or five black women. One white member had to be on the board of directors of the central branch. Checks were constantly established and the guidelines enforced by the board of directors. The black members of the various branches were directed to form a committee of management, which was held responsible for all matters of the local branch. The committee of affiliation acted in an advisory capacity to the committee of management.[24]

The Neighborhood Union became active in the work of the YWCA in 1915. At the conference of the YWCA in Louisville, Kentucky, from October 14 to 16, 1915, it was decided that college chapters would have white student secretaries. Black women from various parts of the South protested the decision. The women took their complaint to the national conference in Cleveland, but were referred back to the southern conference. It was not until the southern conference was held in Richmond in 1917 that black women were given representative administrative and executive jobs.[25]

The YWCA decided also, in 1917, that black women could be trained for work related to the war effort. From $4 million, $200,000 was to be spent to train the black women for war-related services. Hope was assigned to be trained at Camp Upton. Later in 1918, she led the black women of Atlanta at Camp Gordon. The year 1917 also witnessed the organization of the Phillis Wheatley Branch of the YWCA at Atlanta and the conference for "Colored students" at the Spelman Seminary from May 25 to June 4.[26]

Black women, under the leadership of Mary Church Terrell, assistant to the Girls' Department of the National Board of the YWCA, challenged in 1919 the policies and activities of the YWCA. Terrell received letter after letter from black women in southern cities charging that the "Y" was not working with black girls. From a detailed study of eight cities, it was determined that there was a need for a black female "Y" worker who would help to improve the recreational, living conditions, and educational facilities for black women. Some states objected initially to Terrell's plans but reluctantly agreed to honor them after black women applied increased pressure.[27]

Black women still felt they were not being given the proper consideration from the central YWCA. Lucy C. Laney, principal of the Haines Normal and Industrial Institute, stated that black women in the South were calling for representatives on the national board and the right to form their own branches. A petition requesting this was sent to the central YWCA and received positive action in 1925. Black women had to recognize the fact that the YWCA was not willing to allow them to organize and operate as they deemed necessary under the banner of the YWCA. In order to secure decision-making positions within organizations having white members, black women prior to 1925 had to organize their own associations. The black women had recognized that they shared some concerns with the whites; however, they also had concerns which were uniquely different from those of the whites.

In 1892, black women of Washington, D.C., organized the Colored Women's League. They set as their tasks the collection of data about blacks to determine the best methods for blacks to follow and to bring together all units classed as woman's work. James W. Jacks, president of the Missouri Press Association, criticized black women and what he considered their lack of morals in a statement to Florence Belgarnie of London. She sent the statement to the editors of *Woman's Era Magazine*, the organ of the New Era Club. When made aware of the statement, Josephine St. Pierre Ruffin, president of the New Era Club, called a meeting in Boston for black women from July 20 to 31, 1895. Twenty clubs sent representatives who organized the National Federation of Afro-American Women and elected Margaret Murray Washington president. In 1896, the National Federation of Afro-American Women merged with the Colored Women's League of Washington to become the National Association of Colored Women. The federation had established affiliates in the sixteen states, among them Alabama, Georgia, Louisiana, North Carolina, South Carolina, Tennessee, and Virginia.[28]

The association adopted as one of its primary concerns educational opportunities for blacks in the United States. In December 1916 the members advocated the formation of a School Teachers' League in order to help protect the rights of black female teachers. This league was extremely valuable to women in the South, where wages were generally lower and teaching conditions less favorable. The association also instituted industrial homes for girls in the South, day nurseries, boarding homes, and scholarships. By 1920, the membership totaled 300,000 women with chapters in every state, Canada, Liberia, Haiti, and Cuba. Mary B. Talbert of Buffalo, New York, became the presiding officer in 1920.[29]

Another group which became a national organization was the College Alumnae Club of Washington, D.C., founded on March 11, 1910, by ten black women, including Mary Church Terrell. The club had the same structure as the Association of Collegiate Alumnae, for white women. The College Alumnae Club restricted its membership to women with degrees in the arts, sciences, philosophy, literature, or music from any school recognized by the club. The organization established reading clubs for children, provided medical supplies for high schools, encouraged black girls to go to college, and, in 1919, initiated a scholarship program. Lucy Diggs Slowe, the first dean of women at Howard University, encouraged sixty-seven women to meet to broaden the purpose of the College Alumnae Club. On April 24, 1924, the National Association of College Women, largely through the efforts of Dean Slowe, became a permanent organization. Its counterpart was the American Association of University Women, for whites only. The purpose of the National Association of College Women was "to promote a closer union and fellowship among college women for constructive educational work; to study educational conditions in the United States with emphasis upon problems affecting Negroes; to raise educational standards in colleges and universities; to stimulate intellectual attainment among college women; and to arouse within them a consciousness of their responsibility in solving local and national problems."[30]

The educational associations did not change the prevailing attitude concerning the "proper jobs" for black women. During the period of industrialization prior to and through World War I, there was an increase in the interests and activities of women, including those of black women. Black women appeared not to have been concerned with the trade unions which flourished because of this industrial revolution. Mary Church Terrell stated, "It is believed that by founding schools in which Colored girls could be trained to be skilled domestics, we should do more toward solving the labor question as it affects our women, than by using any other means it is in our power to employ."[31] Most of the educated black women who sought professional jobs throughout the period 1895–1925 were teachers. Unskilled black women continued to work as domestics in the homes of whites.

Black women realized that one method of achieving their stated educational goals was to become involved with national movements among whites. One which would have a direct effect upon education was the National American Woman Suffrage Association. The suffrage movement in the United States came of age during the period 1906–13. In 1912, the Progressive party made woman suffrage a part of its plank. Educated black women strongly felt that if they had the vote they could help influence those who were responsible for dictating policies for the southern schools and general issues which affected blacks. The College Alumnae Club was a vigorous supporter of the suffrage movement. By 1912, it was quite apparent that the issue had reached national attention among blacks. *The Crisis* devoted its entire issue in September 1912 to the question. In addition, many articles were included on the suffrage question in *The Crisis* for 1915. In 1912, Mary Terrell was quite active in the movement and was invited twice to address the National American Woman Suffrage Association at its annual convention in Washington. Margaret Washington, elected president of the National Association of Colored Women's Clubs, took a strong stand in favor of suffrage. Adella Hunt Logan, former lady principal of Tuskegee Institute, stated that adequate school facilities were the concern of black mothers, but without a vote they had no voice in educational legislation and no power to see that black children secured a share of public school funds. The only options which seemed available had not proven successful.[32]

National opposition to the advancement of women in general came from at least one educated black male. Kelly Miller, professor at Howard University, did not believe that all women should have the right to vote. "There may be some argument for suffrage for unfortunate females, such as widows and hopeless spinsters, but such status is not contemplated as a normal social relation."[33] Many men, not recognizing that women were their equals, agreed. In August 1920 the Nineteenth Amendment, giving all women the right to vote, was ratified. Nonetheless, black women and men of the South were kept from registering to vote and from the polls through a number of devious means by southern whites, who wanted no change in the system. Black women, through 1925, were not quite able to achieve the desired educational goals through the ballot.

Black women of the South also became involved in the Committee for Interracial Cooperation, a biracial organization that established its base in the South and had as its main goal the improvement of educational and social institutions for blacks. The men who had initiated the committee were reluctant to include women in the organization. They finally agreed to finance a conference for the women which would be held in Memphis. Prior to the Memphis meeting, black women held a second conference after the National Association of Colored Women's Clubs meeting at Tuskegee on July 7, 1920. Ten women remained an extra day at Tuskegee and were joined by two white representatives, Mrs. Luke G. Johnson (first name unavailable) and Estelle Haskins, from the Committee on Racial Relations.[34] The ten black women who remained were Lucy Laney; Margaret Washington, then honorary president of the National Association of Colored Women's Clubs; Jennie B. Moton; Janie P. Barrett from Peak's Turnout, Virginia; Minnie L. Crosthwait, the registrar at Fisk University; Mary Bethune; Lugenia Hope; Marian B. Wilkinson, president of the South Carolina Federation of Colored Women's Clubs; Charlotte Brown; and Mary T. McCrorey from Biddle University at Charlotte, North Carolina.[35]

The black women were asked to prepare a statement concerning current issues in the South: education, suffrage, lynching, and the press. The draft of their statement was submitted to twenty women for correction but only three replied—Moton, Washington, and Hope. Moton and Washington, using the first statement as their basis, sent a reply to the white women marked "for your use only."[36] Hope approved the first draft. Controversy about the content of the statement centered around lynching and suffrage. Hope wanted the women to take a strong stand against lynching. Her colleagues' statement was conciliatory. A final statement was to be presented at the Memphis conference.

After the preliminary plans for the Memphis conference were accepted, the question became which black women would be invited. Margaret Washington and Charlotte Brown had already been invited, and Ruffin and Bethune were under consideration. The white women made it clear that they were only willing to invite black women who would be agreeable to working under the guidelines they established. The women assembled on October 6, 1920, under the title of the Woman's Inter-Racial Conference. Elizabeth Ross Haynes from Fisk, Margaret Washington, and Charlotte Hawkins Brown were to address the group. Jennie Moton was the fourth black woman present.[37]

On the first day the women decided that they would discuss day nurseries and kindergartens, free baby clinics, adequate playgrounds, and recreational facilities. In relation to education, they recommended that a survey of the educational situation in the South be undertaken, more equitable division of school funds be initiated, suitable school buildings be erected and equipment provided, longer school terms be established and higher standards and increased pay for teachers be instituted. The recommendations, largely those drafted in the statement from the Black Women's Conference at Tuskegee, were adopted on October 7, 1920.[38]

Washington's address to the group dealt with two concerns. She felt that the home life of blacks created social problems and that black men and women who lived together without legal ties were the source of evil for the home. She further stated, "All that the older Colored women have, they owe it to southern white women."[39] The influence of her late husband's philosophy was quite apparent. She also stated that she felt that the lack of education was the root of many problems and evils for blacks. She called for formally educated teachers in order to promote better schools. Clinging to the industrial education concept, she urged the teaching of agriculture, cooking, and handicrafts. Industrial education would also motivate blacks to remain in the rural areas. After her address, the whites present raised several questions but Washington's chief response was, "All the Colored person asks, is a chance to be and do better."[40] Washington told the whites what they believed and also what they wanted to hear. It would be up to other blacks at the conference to challenge her beliefs.

Whites at the conference questioned the educated black woman's relationship to those blacks who had not achieved as much. Haynes responded by saying, "I do feel that the white women in most places are making the mistake of appealing to us—I mean the more intelligent element of the Colored women. We are not always in touch with the masses of the people."[41] Through this statement, Haynes articulated an old problem: separation from the masses was not confined to black professional males. The reality of social conditions in the South for blacks dictated a certain degree of separation between the educated and the masses. Yet, some blacks could not afford to ignore the fact that certain problems existed for all blacks. Haynes alluded to the commonality of certain problems for all blacks during her speech to the assembly at the morning session on October 8, 1920. She explained what it meant to be black and to suffer under segregation and the Jim Crow laws.

Charlotte Brown began her talk by stating, "You heard from Mrs. Washington yesterday afternoon, who represents the conservative type of our Negro woman in this country."[42] Since Brown felt that others viewed her as being a little radical, she hastened to point out that she was sincere in all that she said. On her way to the conference she was asked to leave the sleeper on the train and go to the day coach, which was considered by many whites the place for blacks to ride. Twelve white men demanded that she do this. She honored their demand and became determined to tell of her experience at the conference. Brown was thus able to support the statements made by Haynes regarding the commonality of certain problems for all blacks.

The public desired to see copies of the addresses given by the black women at Memphis. There was, however, a mild controversy brewing. Should the addresses and the statement prepared at Tuskegee be released to the general public? After revision, a third copy was prepared. Moton and Washington refused to sign it. The final copy, however, carried their signatures. The statement on lynching contained the essence of Hope's thoughts, while the statement on education was not drastically changed. The third draft, including Hope's statement on lynching, urged support for better educational facilities, and had a strongly worded introductory statement. The women stated that a democratic society could not be maintained unless all children were educated. Neglect and poverty were directly parallel with ignorance and crime. In the final statement, signed by Brown, Wilkinson, Laney, McCrorey, Washington, Moton, Hope, Bethune, Crosthwait, and Barrett, the introductory statement was omitted.[43]

A decision was made on March 29, 1921, to permit the blacks to become permanent members of the central committee partly because of the continual controversy over the statement issued by the black women. From June 28 to 30, the Southern Federation of Colored Women's Clubs assembled in Atlanta to affirm their position on the released statement. They still objected to the statement on lynching. Led by Hope, the group wished to submit a stronger statement. Mrs. Moton and Mrs. Washington were not present.[44]

Those black female activists who were willing to challenge the existing order in the South quickly found that their approach would not always be the one to which white women would agree. On October 7, 1921, the Committee for Inter-Racial Cooperation met at the YWCA auditorium in Atlanta. The only black person there was Charlotte Brown. In her comments at the meeting she stated that she desired to be of service to both races. She suggested more—and a different type—of contact with blacks. Brown was aware that until the educated black female was respected for her opinions and efforts, no true cooperation would be possible. At the end of Brown's address, Mrs. Luke Johnson stated that the Committee would attempt to bring the black and white women together.[45]

The combined efforts of black and white women working for common concerns would not become a reality until after 1925. The period 1895–1925, witnessed, however, the beginning of cooperation among the races and sexes. Black women had attempted to work with whites but found it easier to work alone, to develop and strengthen their own organization, and, in later years, to merge with whites when necessary.

Black women during the period 1895-1925 were positive forces for change. Although generally accepting the roles defined for them by the larger society and by black men, black women, dissatisfied with prevailing conditions in the South, successfully initiated programs and clubs which not only provided services for the masses but also enabled educated black women to further their educational goals. Organizations on the local level were partly successful because of the membership size and commonalities among the women. The national organizations were not as effective. Once organizations broadened their focus and membership, conflicts appeared, often because of personal philosophies and rivalries. Women like Hope and Terrell withdrew from those organizations having conflicts but continued to work for the betterment of the race. In general, however, the educated black woman worked to improve the condition of the race.

# DAPHNE DUVAL HARRISON

# 5

## BLACK WOMEN IN THE BLUES TRADITION

The blues has been chronicled by many who have been interested in its poetic structure, its literary content, its graphic depiction of black life, and its legendary characters. Sociological, literary, and musicological treatises have firmly established blues as a valid folk art. Writers like Baraka (Leroi Jones) and Charles Keil consider the blues as the only indigenous art form of the United States of America. This essay, however, is not concerned with arguing about the validity of the blues as an art form. The questions raised here are concerned with the image of black women performers in the early development of the blues, particularly during what is now referred to as the "classic" blues era (1920-33).

Superficial references to black women blues performers are usually found sprinkled amidst the essays on the men performers in the field. These items usually mention the performer's name and the musical groups with whom she recorded and performed. However, a search of the literature revealed a dearth of information about most of the outstanding women performers of a given era.[1] Many names are listed, but little or no substantive data about their life circumstances are presented. Several very fine discographies offer listings of many of the recordings, but these generally had only promotional materials, which cannot be considered as valid sources. Thus my need to know better the black women who sang the blues led me to these questions:

1. What circumstances influenced black women to pursue the itinerant life of a tent show and theater performer?
2. How were black women blues performers perceived by other segments of the black population?
3. How did their music reflect their lives?
4. How did their music shape the blues in general?

# CRAZY BLUES

By PERRY BRADFORD

MAMIE SMITH AND HER JAZZ HOUNDS

Get this number for your phonograph on Okeh Record No. 4169

PUBLISHED BY
PERRY BRADFORD
MUSIC PUB. CO.
1547 BROADWAY, N. Y. C.

**Mamie Smith and Her Jazz Hounds**

The answers are only slowly coming because of the difficulty in obtaining primary as well as secondary sources. Noted blues authorities like Paul Oliver, Samuel Charters, and Harry Oster either were not much concerned about the role of black women performers or had the same difficulty as this writer in searching the literature.[2] It is my belief that the former is probably the case, because these writers did intensive field research. In fact, they interviewed such persons as Victoria Spivey when seeking data about male performers. For this reason, many laymen assume that women began performing the blues during that period between 1920 and 1933 which is called the "classic" blues era.[3] This is unfortunate because it gives a very limited view of black women blues artists. Also, there is a concomitant implication that Delta and country blues were mainly the domain of men like Big Bill Broonzy, Blind Lemon Jefferson, and Son House.

I approach this research with the assumption that there were forces other than personal aspirations which influenced the careers of singers such as Mamie Smith, Bessie Smith, Ma Rainey, and Lucille Hegamin. Eileen Southern, in *Music of Black Americans* (1971), implies that racism influenced the choice of an entertainment career by many attractive young black women.[4] That is, at the turn of the twentieth century, the combination of physical freedom for blacks with economic oppression propelled many blacks into itinerant job seeking while at the same time leaving many women to support their families with domestic labor. The enactment of Jim Crow laws had an effect upon black entertainment in that the roles which were more appealing to segregated white audiences cast black males as comedians rather than serious entertainers. The mainly white audiences were not expected to respond warmly to vaudevillian acts that cast black males in other than comedic slapstick routines or as instrumentalists. These same shows featured several beautiful black women, preferably the light-skinned mulatto types, as singers and dancers. It is interesting to note that the counterpart Gay Nineties–type shows featured both highly attractive white males and females. This paradox of what was expected of black entertainers and what they expected to provide created the background for many young, beautiful, talented black women, who entered the world of road shows. In their attempt to escape the poverty and hardship of black life in the rural South they sought escape through the seeming glamour and opportunity for fame in the segregated world of the Theatre Owners Booking Agency (TOBA).

Another aspect of this trend was the upsurge of houses of ill-repute in the larger cities, which offered the best entertainment for their clientele, affluent white males. The Storyville area of New Orleans flourished with elaborately furnished, plush saloons featuring talented black musicians whose music was usually hot or sentimental.[5] Besides these houses, the bars and saloons of New Orleans, Memphis, Kansas City, Saint Louis, and Chicago offered steady work for some of the women. Their music is vivid with the imagery of the tough life, marked by whiskey, two-timing men, or nostalgia.

Unfortunately, some women began as street singers while quite young, singing for a few coins a day. Bessie Smith began this way, though she eventually rose to fame as a recording star. Her first professional appearance was in Ma Rainey's "Rabbit Foot Minstrels," which toured the TOBA circuit regularly throughout the South.[6] Bessie was in her early teens when she was "discovered," so that she escaped a poverty-stricken existence quite early. The TOBA was considered to be quite hard on its performers, so that it was called "Tough on Black Artists." Bessie was discovered by Frank Walker while on the circuit and began a stormy career which has developed into the Bessie Smith legend. Although Bessie is probably the best-known performer of the "classic" era, it was Perry Bradford's insistence on having Mamie Smith, an unknown young black woman, recorded on that fateful day in February 1920 that started the whole thrust of blues race records.[7] Where did the likes of Mamie begin their careers?

George Mitchell, in his brief photographic essay of the Mississippi blues country, found two performers, Rosa Lee Hill and Jessie Mae Brooks, her niece. Rosa was born about the time Bessie Smith had begun a singing career with Ma Rainey's "Rabbit Foot Minstrels." Much like Bessie, she began her musical career at eight or nine years of age. She was taught the guitar by her father, Sid Hemphill, a talented musician who played for local parties, festivities, and church gatherings. His ability to play several instruments and many types of music, depending on the requirements of his client, gave Rosa a rich background of music that she clung to in spite of the poverty her family endured during her developing years. Her formal education ended at the age of twelve because of the high cost of books. Her warm relationship with her father and sister was a strong influence on her life and served to provide the mainstay of her very limited career. She remained married to one man, a farmer with whom she sharecropped, and with whom she cared for her relatives' children because she and her husband never had any children of their own.

Upon marriage, Rosa ended her professional singing career. She continued to sing for herself, but she regarded the blues as bad songs that came from her mouth, not her heart, when she was down. And she had many years of near starvation, yet she commented that thinking of a good song, which usually was a church song, brought tears to her eyes.

Rosa Lee Hill's life suggests that the mores of the rural areas where she lived accepted blues performers, male or female, as home folk who could share their talents. According to the firsthand accounts in Mitchell, she was loved and respected by her husband, family, and friends. Maybe because her performing was limited to home and nearby, she was never regarded as a stage person, with all the negative connotations many blacks attributed to that occupation.

Her own classification of blues as bad, but somehow necessary to relieve or relive the misery of poverty, reflects vividly how she used the blues for self-expression. Rosa probably had little influence on the shape of blues in the larger world of entertainment, but surely her renown as a guitar player and singer influenced younger local musicians, such as her niece, Jessie Mae Brooks, until Rosa's death in 1968.[8]

I chose Rosa Hill as the first person to discuss because she probably is prototypical of a large number of black women who still live in rural areas of the South, who may have been blues performers much like the male country bluesmen, Blind Lemon Jefferson and Son House. Why were they overlooked in recordings and literature?

By contrast, Ida Cox, born in Knoxville, Tennessee, in 1889, began traveling with the "Rabbit Foot Minstrels" when she was fourteen years old. Her career reflects a pattern which Oliver generalizes to most of the "classic" blues singers—that is, early apprenticeship in the rough, tough life of the tent shows. She traveled throughout the South with Rabbit Foot and Silas Green for many years and later formed her own "Raisin' Cain" Company. Fifty or more years of performing and recording did not yield enough data to inspire Oliver to discuss any more than with whom she recorded. Her style certainly influenced other singers, because that nasal quality is present in more contemporary artists such as the late Dinah Washington and Esther Phillips. Yet, Ida surely must have embodied more than an entertainment personality. What should we assume from her lyrics?

> I don't want no Northern yellow,
>     no Northern Black or brown (repeat)
> Southern men will stick by you
>     when the Northern men
>     can't be found.[9]

Do they portray her disenchantment with northern men and life accurately? Maybe, maybe not; a description of her career by Victoria Spivey in Stewart-Baxter's book indicates she was an astounding woman both on and off stage. She was formidable as a performer because of her great voice and style and as a composer of some of the best blues of that era, e.g., "Moaning the Blues" recorded by Spivey. She made plenty of money, wore fine clothes, and lived as she pleased while touring with her own Raisin' Cain company during the twenties and thirties. She continued performing through the 1930s, although her last recording was made for Paramount in 1929. Her most popular number, "Wild Women Don't Have the Blues," may have typified her feelings.

Cox came out of semi-retirement for two recording dates in 1939 and 1940 and was relatively successful. However, an attempt to revive some interest in her as a performer in 1961 resulted in a recording of poor quality because of the loss of her sense of timing and voice.[10]

Big Bill Broonzy, the outstanding male blues singer, said singers like Ida, Bessie Smith, "Ma" Rainey, and Memphis Minnie sang the blues because of the trouble "sweetback papas" gave them.[11] Ma Rainey's lyrics reflected that idea when she sang,

> People have the different blues and think they're
>   mighty sad
> But blues about a man is the worst
>   I ever had. . . .

Or Alice Moore's

> My man, my man, leaves me so low down, [repeat]
>   Everything I do, seems like to me is wrong.
> I love my man, but he loves somebody else [repeat]
>   I think I'm a damn fool to keep on worrying myself.[12]

Or Bessie Tucker, saying:

> Hey, hey, hey, what's the matter with my man today [repeat]
>   I asked him if he loved me and he walked away.[13]

The titles of recordings also support Broonzy's analysis of the blues lyrics of women singers: for example, Memphis Minnie on Checker singing "Broken Heart" and "Mean Mistreater Blues," Big Mama Thornton's "All Fed Up" and "I Ain't No Fool" on Peacock; Ora Alexander's "Men Sure Are Deceiving," and Bessie Smith's "Empty Bed Blues."[14]

If lyrics are the key to understanding the psychic orientation of a performer, how do we account for the wide range of topics recorded by Bessie Smith? Charters, Oliver, and Cook[15] each remark about the unevenness in the quality of the material Bessie sang. In many instances she overrode the poor material by her penchant for careful, excellent recording quality.

A glance at record titles might provide a clue to the topics of interest to the buying public but does not guarantee that the singer was reflecting her own feelings. It is probably wiser to assume that life experiences tempered the expression of the performer as much as did the lyrics. Willie Mae "Big Mama" Thornton is quoted by Shaw: "My singing comes from my experience . . . my own feeling . . . I never had no one to teach me. I taught myself everything."[16] Alberta Hunter said, "To me, the blues are almost religious . . . almost sacred—when we sing the blues, we're singing out of our own hearts . . . our feelings. . . . Maybe we're hurt and just can't answer back."[17]

A look at the lives of performers who were born at the turn of the century reveals their common environment and socioeconomic background. Poverty forced many upon the streets to seek outlet through musical expression. Bessie Smith, Ida Cox, Gertrude ("Ma") Rainey, Alberta Hunter, Victoria Spivey, and "Memphis" Minnie Douglas were all performing professionally by their sixteenth birthdays. This fact alone indicated that the attitudes about a "proper" life for such young women (as viewed by them) was in conflict with those of the general black community, which regarded theatrical life as sinful for "nice young ladies."

Bessie Smith began singing for coins on the streets of Tennessee. Legend clouds the circumstances of Bessie's discovery by Ma Rainey. Nevertheless, she was a regular member of Rabbit Foot Minstrels under Ma's tutelage at the beginning of her career. Fortunately for Bessie, Ma Rainey had the warm kind of personality which allowed her to teach Bessie as much as she could and then let her seek independence. The literature has conflicting stories of Bessie's attitude toward persons who helped her. She seemed to be driven toward self-destruction, yet she had an uncanny perception of her star power, and she used it to the hilt in her performances, both public and private. She was said to be generous to a fault; yet, she was vindictive for seemingly trivial reasons. She was threatened by the presence of other entertainers (her feud with Ethel Waters is legendary). Because her childhood of extreme poverty made it easy to take to the streets to earn pennies, she may have developed a keen sense of competition with others in her field.

Her extreme ranges in mood caused her to make unwise business decisions which resulted in great financial losses. This same reason may have hastened the final collapse of a shaky marriage to a man who did not have the psychic strength to sustain a relationship with such a volatile personality.

Bessie's penchant for the dramatic, which was nurtured in her early school days, earned her the title "Empress of the Blues."[18] She was

statuesque and good-looking, and she dominated her audiences when she
began her moaning. She maintained that image even through the awful
decline of her career brought on by a combination of heavy drinking,
high living, and the perfidy of public taste. According to Cook, it is to her
credit that she maintained absolute integrity in her recordings—as if she
knew she was leaving them for posterity.[19] Her fine artistry influenced
and mesmerized musicians of many inclinations, like Mahalia Jackson,
who never sang the blues but listened to Bessie's recordings and acknowledged their influence on her singing.[20] A *Who's Who* of American
musicians would include many of those she influenced: Louis Armstrong,
Bix Beiderbecke, Sidney Bechet, Ethel Waters, Billie Holiday, Mezz
Mezzrow, Fletcher Henderson and other. Robert Hayden evoked her image
in his ode "Homage to the Empress of the Blues."

> Because there was a man somewhere in a candystripe silk shirt gracile
> and dangerous as a jaguar and because a woman moaned for him
> in sixty-watt gloom and mourned him Faithless Love Twotiming
> Love Oh Love Oh Careless Aggravating Love
> She came out on stage in yards of pearls, emerging like a favorite
> scenic view, flashed her golden smile and sang. . .[21]

An apparent contrast to Bessie Smith was Gertrude ("Ma") Rainey
(nee Pridgett), who was born a decade earlier than Bessie in Columbus,
Georgia.[22] Ma Rainey's early marriage to Will Rainey occurred after she
won a local talent show in Columbus.[23] They formed a vaudeville part-
nership that toured the South. There she absorbed the blues from her
close contact with people. She became known as the "Mother of the
Blues" because of her warm personality, her boisterous manner of singing,
and her stocky, squat, homely looks.[24] Her audiences reacted to her with
affection because she maintained a bond with them through her understanding of the blues as she sang, for example, "Yonder Comes the Blues":

> I worry all day, I worry all night,
>     Every time my man comes home he wants to fuss and fight,
> When I pick up the paper to try to read the news,
>     Just when I'm satisfied, yonder comes the blues.
>
> I went down the river each and every day,
>     Trying to keep from throwing myself away,
> I walked and I walked 'til I wore out my shoes,
>     I can't walk no further, yonder comes the blues. . .
>
> People have the different blues and think they're mighty sad,
>     But the blues about a man is the worst I ever had.

I been disgusted and all confused,
Every time I look around, yonder comes the blues.[25]

Ma Rainey recorded extensively, but she never became a part of the northern urban blues centers. She kept the folk atmosphere of southern blues through the continued use of jug bands, kazoos, and barrelhouse pianists. She performed with such productions as those of Silas Green, Al Gaines, and C. W. Parks, as well as in her own shows. Although she was referred to as squat, ugly, and homely, persons who heard her perform agreed she knew how to sing the blues. Sterling Brown is quoted by Paul Oliver as saying that Ma knew the people because she was of them, simple and direct.[26] Brown's poem "Ma Rainey" captures the feeling eloquently:

When Ma Rainey Comes to town,
    Folks from anyplace Miles aroun'
From Cape Girardeau, Poplar Bluff
    Flocks in to hear Ma do her stuff,
Comes flivvering in Or riding mules,
    Or packed in trains, Picknickin' fools
That what it's like, Fo' miles on down
    To New Orleans delta An' Mobile town.
When Ma Hits Anywheres aroun'
    Dey comes to hear Ma Rainey from de little river settlements
From blackbottom cornrows and from lumber camps
    Dey stumble in de halls, jes' a-laughin' an' a-cracklin',
Cheerin' lak roaring water, lak wind in river swamps.
    An' some jokers keep deir laughs a-goin' in de crowded aisles,
An' some folks sits dere waiting wid deir aches an' miseries
Till Ma comes out before dem a-smilin' gold-toofed smiles. . .[27]

Stewart-Baxter suggests that her penchant for spangled dress, jewelry, and young men did not complete the picture of her. Her outspoken sternness was a cloak for warmth and generosity. She was a fantastic performer, well-loved by her southern audiences even when northerners stopped buying her "out of fashion" records. She eventually bought two theaters in Georgia and remained there until her death at about fifty years of age, when she was buried in her family plot.[28]

Here we see a picture of contrasts: the glamorous tragedy-laden life of Bessie Smith, "the Empress of the Blues," northern style, on one hand; on the other, Gertrude ("Ma") Rainey, "the Queen of the Blues," southern blues—successful and tough, maybe, but resilient and attached to her roots. Can we speculate that Ma's confidence in herself was supported and developed because she maintained her ties with her people; because she remained one of them and identified with her audiences?

On the other hand can we assume that Bessie's striving for stardom and a pinnacle of fame occupied by only herself also separated her from the only connections with reality for a performer—the people? Could this possibly have been the source for her increasing discontent, which led to behavior that resulted in Sidney Bechet's description of her as "a hell of a fine woman . . . but she had this meanness in her!"[29] Once more the question of life influencing music, which reflects life, is left to speculation.

One of the artists who was influenced by Bessie Smith was Sippie Wallace (nee Thomas). Stewart-Baxter describes her piano playing as rolling and powerful like the music of her native state, Texas.[30] This is assuredly so, as one may be able to discern if one is fortunate enough to hear her early records. She came from a strong musical background; her brother, Hersal, was a fine pianist and composer; an older brother, George, eventually became a publisher; and her niece, Hociel, established herself as an accomplished pianist and singer.[31]

In an interview, Wallace said she would secretly listen to records by Bessie, Mamie Smith, and Ethel Waters at her uncle's house because her mother disapproved of the blues. She used these listening sessions as the basis for her training to eventually become a recording star. She was so intent upon a performing career that she risked the ire of her mother and followed the male members of her family into what became a life-long career. According to Stewart-Baxter, Sippie went to New York for the first time in 1923 and then toured for many years on the infamous TOBA circuit. He says she did not mind the hard life, because singing and playing were what she had to do. Although she claims she was younger than Bessie and Mamie Smith, she began her recording career in the twenties just as they did. Her singing and playing were showcased with such talented musicians as Louis Armstrong, her brother Hersal Thomas, and Lil Hardin, Armstrong's wife.[32]

A composer and pianist of no mean talent, Wallace reactivated her career after many years of retirement when Victoria Spivey mentioned her to an agency that was organizing an annual blues package tour.[33] She now lives in Detroit and continues to perform. Her recent engagements included a blues festival in Highland Park, Michigan, in the spring of 1974, and performances in Boston and Washington with Roosevelt Sykes as her back-up musician in the fall of 1974. Time has taken its toll, for her voice and body are afflicted with age. Sippie's performance with Bonnie Raitt of two of her old numbers did have glimmers of her brash younger days, but were more a reflection of things past. The mostly white, quite young audience paid to see Bonnie, so they were not in a receptive mood for an old lady whom they knew not.

Sippie's compositions and performances, like those of many artists of her era, reflect a variety of thoughts. She moans about the loss of her man in "Special Delivery Blues":

> I looked through the window, as the train was passing by,
> Ran to the window as the train was passing by
> Lord, he gives me the blues so bad I tho't I would die.[34]

"You Gonna Need My Help" warns her man of his possible regrets if he gets out of line and she decides to leave him. Her composition, "Caledonia," however, deals with a hard-headed woman who did not heed her mother's advice.[35]

Sippie still sings, plays, and composes the blues, but she has lost the vitality of her younger years. She appears occasionally with Bonnie Raitt on tours in the Midwest and Northeast, but more in deference to her early works, which Bonnie likes to perform.

A blues performer whose style was more like the bluesmen, Big Bill Broonzy, Son House, and Willie McTell, was "Memphis" Minnie McCoy. She was born in Algiers, Louisiana, but she became famous on the streets of Memphis as Kid Douglas due to her prowess as a guitarist.[36] She was playing and singing in and out of saloons on Beale Street by age fifteen. Columbia Records discovered her and took her to Chicago. Her musical career began as a result of a banjo given her by her father when she was ten years old. Her early career reflects the same hard itinerary as mentioned earlier. She traveled throughout the South for several years with Ringling Brothers' circus.[37] Indicative of the destructive forces developing around children of that era, which led to many of them becoming hoboes and wandering around the country, is her recording:

> Lay down at night, trying to play my hand,
> Through the window, out stepped a man,
> I didn't know no better, oh boy, in ma
>    girlish days.
>        . . .
> I flagged a train, didn't have a dime.
> Trying to run away from that home of mine.
> I didn't know no better, oh boy, in ma
>    girlish days.[38]

Minnie recorded later than the women mentioned earlier, yet her style remained a strong, hard-driving one, much like that of men performers like Bill Broonzy. Her voice was considered as loud and strong as a man's.

In fact, she and Broonzy competed in a blues contest about 1933; he lost to her performances of "Me and My Chauffeur" and "Looking the World Over." Broonzy says he tried to win by encouraging her to drink too much, but she played him under.[39] Broonzy is quoted as saying "Memphis Minnie can make a guitar cry, moan, talk, and whistle the blues."

Minnie's recording career included releases with two of her husbands. With one of these, "Kansas City" Joe McCoy, she recorded for a period of over six years. While married to her third husband, Ernest Lawler (Little Son Joe), she made more recordings, including the quite sensitive and tender "When You Love Me":

> I see your face before me all through the night and day
> Oh, all through the night and day,
> But I still love you in the same old way.[40]

She was noted for helping younger performers by giving Blue Monday parties at which they could stage their talent. Rosetta "Sister" Tharpe was probably influenced by Memphis Minnie's hard picking guitar style. Sources conflict on the number of men she married. None indicates children.

The TOBA circuit shows, the minstrel shows, the traveling circuses in the early part of the century depended on audiences that were mainly white, mainly male. This created a sociological background which encouraged beautiful, talented, black women to endure the insults, degradation, and hardship of tent show life. Why did they do it? Because the money was good, and they could escape the poverty of black life in the rural South. Also, because the black male did not have the opportunities to find jobs, black females sought work or new mates to maintain families.

Oliver discusses the reflection of this phenomenon in the many blues lyrics that graphically portray the desperation of lives destroyed by share cropping. Ida Cox's "Worn Out Daddy Blues" tells of the misery and hard choices of a woman whose man cannot fulfill his role as husband and father:

> The time has come for us to part,
> I ain't goin' to cry, it won't break my heart,
> Cause I'm through with you and I hope you don't feel hurt.
>
> You're like an old horseshoe that's had its day
> You're like an old horseshoe I must throw away,
> I'm through with you and I hope you don't feel hurt.

You ain't got no money, you're down and broke,
You're just an old has-been like a worn-out joke,
So I'm through with you and I hope you don't feel hurt.[41]

The converse of the predicament of men in the rural South was the availability of jobs for women in the North. The aggression of women singers might be related to their position in northern Negro society between World Wars I and II. They could find jobs when men could not; but men, though economically weak, exalted their sexual prowess. Lyrics of men singers are full of imagery like "I'm a rooting groundhog, babe; and I roots everywhere I go."[42] On the other hand, women tended to alternate between moods of defensive hardness and lavish tenderness. Mary Johnson, from Saint Louis, earned the name "Signifyin' Mary" because of the suspicion of men expressed on many of her recordings. Georgia White, a singer and pianist from rural Georgia recorded with Jimmy Noone in Chicago. Her strong voice had a good range and tough quality, which Oliver considered appropriate for urban lyrics about prostitution, lesbianism, or similar themes. Sara Martin sang "Mean Tight Mama":

Now my hair is nappy and I don't wear no clothes of silk [repeat]
But the cow that's black and ugly has often got the sweetest milk.

Now when a man starts giving I'm tighter than a pair of shoes [repeat]
I'm a mean tight mama, with my mean tight mama blues.[43]

Edith Johnson's "Nickel's Worth of Liver" was downright braggadocio:

I got a man upstairs, one downstairs,
    one across the street,
You got your eyes wide open, but you're
    sound asleep.

Ma Rainey is said to have recorded "Hustlin' Blues," out of character for her in its allusions to prostitution:

It's rainin' out here, and tricks ain't
    walkin' tonight [repeat]
I'm going home, I know I've got to fight.

        . . .

I ain't made no money, and he dared me
    to go home [repeat]
Judge, I told him he better leave me alone.

        . . .

> Oh, judge, tell him I'm through [repeat]
> I'm tired of this life, that's why I brought
> him to you.[44]

So, again, the conflict between man and woman spawns lyrics which reflect the misery and degradation imposed by a society unwilling to accept a group of people.

One of the ironies of "Hustlin' Blues" is that it was composed by Thomas Dorsey, the grand old man of gospel music fame. He was a blues pianist on the Saint Louis-Kansas City circuit before a personal tragedy influenced his move to religious music.[45]

New Orleans blues performers emerged from a different set of circumstances from those discussed previously. The infamous Storyville and Bourbon Streets housed different types of employment opportunities from the bars and barbershops of Memphis, Saint Louis, and Kansas City. These were the lavish saloons and bordellos that housed beautiful octoroons and mulattos for the pleasure of wealthy white males. At one such bordello, Countess Willie Piazza had the distinction of hiring the first pianist to entertain her customers. Here, Ann Cook, one of New Orleans's first blues singers, launched her career.[46] Another such performer was Lizzie Miles, born Elizabeth Mary Landreaux in 1895 in New Orleans. She recorded with such eminent New Orleans and Chicago jazzmen as King Oliver and "Jelly Roll" Morton.

Danny Barker, whose wife Lu was an outstanding performer in her own right, mentioned other women who performed during that period. Unfortunately, he did not describe in any detail the quality and extent of their performances. He did state that the practice of many New Orleans groups of performing on the streets may have been a constraint on women who were musicians.[47] Although many may have played piano, that was frowned upon as a possible career medium. Some women overlooked these constaints and sought entertainment careers anyway. Among them were Dolly Adams, Blanche Thomas, Jeanette Kimball, Billie Pierce (Preservation Hall Jazz Band), Sweet Emma Barrett (Heritage Hall) and Olivia Charlot.[48] Sweet Emma and Billie continued performing until their recent deaths. Charlot indicated that her career was restrained by men in the entertainment world, who refused to hire her as a pianist with all-male bands. She also had difficulty in obtaining membership in the musicians' local in the early days of her career during the late twenties and early thirties. She eventually overcame those obstacles and became an active officer in the local. She is still an active performer who has adapted to the demands of the industry by switching to electronic instruments. With pride she relates the compliments she receives for "getting so much sound from that little thing."[49] Charlot and Barker are sharing their heritage by giving special jazz concerts for children in New Orleans each spring.

Edith Wilson, a classic blues singer from Chicago, has indicated that her life was free of economic strain. She came from a well-educated family in Louisville.[50] Her recordings and performances were not limited to blues. She was a vaudeville performer of no mean talent who was well recorded. She is enjoying a renewed career and appears in concerts throughout the country, living comfortably in Chicago. She feels her family was supportive of her career aspirations. Her appearance as Aunt Jemima on early commercials was criticized as demeaning, according to Stewart-Baxter.[51]

Helen Humes's socioeconomic background and career pattern resembles that of Wilson. Although one of her earliest recordings was a Victoria Spivey blues, she did not continue as a blues singer only. Her singing career was enlarged through her performances with big bands like Count Basie's. Stylistically she is a blues-jazz artist who continued to develop as American music changed over the past twenty-five years. She came out of a self-imposed retirement in 1974 to perform again.[52]

The commercial recording industry capitalized on the economics of racism when it established race records for the purpose of exploiting the black market. During this period women were transplanted from small southern towns to big urban centers. This migration may have resulted in disorientation for some. Classic blues became a woman-oriented idiom which often capitalized on lyrics that were explicit in their sexual connotations. Although the records were aimed toward the race market and were heavily purchased by blacks, they were bought by whites, too. The image of the black woman is thus again projected as in the bordellos, and previously on plantations, as a sex object, alluring and suggestive. Though her own feelings of depression, misery, and heartbreak were aimed toward her black men, she was being exploited by whites for economic purposes. The crash of the recording industry resulted in the end of many careers of singers who were billed as the "hottest" thing on the market. Ironically, such a company as Columbia, which was financially rescued by the vocal chords of Bessie Smith, did not credit her for its success.[53]

The success stories are revealed through the proliferation of names in discographies of blues recordings and in little vignettes of writers. They include persons like Lucille Hegamin, Edith Wilson, Victoria Spivey, and Sippie Wallace, who lived long enough to reflect on that era and to pass on information to others. They include Rosa Hill, who was born and died in the rural South and who performed only for her people in small social gatherings. They include the talented like Willie ("Big

Mama") Thornton, exploited by mediocre white performers like Elvis Presley, who launched his multi-million dollar career on a piece which was composed for her, "Hound Dog," but for which she receives a pittance in royalties. Lil Green composed "Blow Top Blues," but it was Peggy Lee who became famous.

The black woman blues artist has been influenced by sociological conditions which bound her inextricably in a paradox of glitter, glamour, fame, and sudden wealth, coupled with ostracism, loneliness, exploitation, and sudden poverty. Her name might be that of Billie Holiday, Aretha Franklin, Georgia White, Memphis Minnie, Esther Phillips, Lena Horne, or the others who have slipped through history unknown—but who have sung the blues as they waited for a man who would not return; as they pained over another child with not enough food to feed it; as they watched the world become dirtier, uglier, and meaner in its treatment of black people.

The black woman blues performer reflects the lives of black women by using tension creatively and by producing a proliferation of imagery, expressiveness, and music which continues to have impact upon all of us, directly or indirectly. Many have associated the blues with the shady side of life. According to Nicholas, however, "the blues . . . gets down—portrays the harsh reality of the black experience in America."[54] He continues:

The blues does not offer an escape (like say, suicide, drugs, or astrology) from the hard, bitter, day-to-day struggle to survive and, ultimately, to prevail, but deals with what is real—as Richard Wright wrote, "a lusty, lyrical realism charged with taut sensibility."[55]

The black women in the blues tradition used the tension they lived with creatively by responding with that "lusty, lyrical realism." They deserve, therefore, recognition and understanding as people who lived through that hard realism but who managed to share themselves artistically in spite of it.

Some tentative inferences which may be drawn from these data are that black women blues singers (1) were exploited to benefit the recording industry through their race market; (2) were discriminated against because of their sex and their race; (3) developed a unique form of artistic expression as a result of oppressive societal conditions; and (4) responded differentially to those conditions based upon the socioeconomic background of their families. Further research utilizing additional primary sources is needed to better assess the speculations set forth by this writer. The importance of this era is noted by many authors who have studied the Harlem Renaissance. Research on this segment of that era would add a dimension to the study of American history and culture which is presently missing. Since oral history is affected by time, age and mental alertness of subjects, and difficulty of identifying and locating legitimate sources, research like this should move forward swiftly. The contribution to the fields of knowledge on black women, music, and mental health would be enriching.

# ANDREA BENTON RUSHING

# 6

## IMAGES OF BLACK WOMEN IN AFRO-AMERICAN POETRY

first
a woman should
be
a woman *first,*
but
if she's *black,* really black
and a woman
that's special, that's real special.[1]

"The Negro," Richard Wright said, "is America's metaphor." In a way, black women function as metaphors for salient aspects of the black experience in this strange and terrible land. The symbolism which surrounds them creates a paradox: images of black women in Afro-American poetry are both varied and narrow. They afford a greater range of types than the two-stop Mammy-Sapphire syndrome of films, but, except on rare occasions, they fail to portray the multifaceted nature of the black woman in America. Although audience, the author's sex, and the prevailing literary conventions are all contributing factors, the main reason we do not see the richness and variety of black women reflected in Afro-American poetry is that women often symbolize aspects of black life that are valued by the race. As Dunbar says:

> The women of a race should be its pride;
> We glory in the strength our mothers had,
> We glory that this strength was not denied
> To labor bravely, nobly, and be glad.[2]

That usually unconscious symbolic thrust has been something of a strait-jacket. It is not so much that there are, in Waring Cuney's words, "No Images," but rather that the images only rarely reflect the full reality.

---

Based on an article which originally appeared in *Black World,* September 1975.

**Gwendolyn Brooks**

The most prevalent image of black women in Afro-American poetry is the image of mother. We find it in early poetry like Frances Harper's "Eliza Harris" and "The Slave Auction," in Helene Johnson's "The Mother's Rock," in John Wesley Holloway's "Black Mammies," and in Jessie Fauset's "Oriflamme." We also find it in recent poetry like Ed Sprigg's "my beige mom." Almost all the images of mother revolve around her strength under stress. This is in contrast to African literature, where, according to Wilfred Cartey, the West Indian Africanist, mother and the earth of Africa are one symbol, and mother is the cushion from troubled and chaotic conditions who manifests affection, possessiveness, and shrewd practicality: an emblem of strength and support.[3] Cartey cites the Guinean author Camara Laye: "She was Mother. She belonged to me. With her everything was always all right."[4] It is rare to find an Afro-American mother likened to the earth; this may be because we are not still a peasant people or because, after the agonies of slavery and Reconstruction, we are too bitter about the land to use it as a nurturing metaphor. In the Afro-American tradition, mother is not a cushion but the impetus and example for perseverance in a hostile world. (There are, though, suffering mothers like the one portrayed in Sterling Brown's "Maumee Ruth," where the dying woman has lost her children to the city, cocaine, and gin.) Langston Hughes's "Mother to Son," with its brilliant staircase metaphor, is the best-known example of this.

The most extensive treatment of mother in black poetry comes from master poet Gwendolyn Brooks, whose gallery includes Emmett Till's strangely passive mother; Mrs. Sallie Smith, the "prudent partridge"[5] mother of nine; Mrs. Martin, who disowns her son when he makes Rosa Brown pregnant; and Jessie Mitchell's vindictive yellow mother, who, ill, comforts herself comparing her "exquisite yellow youth"[6] to the hard fate she predicts for her black daughter. Two of Brooks's most memorable figures are the dazed and doomed speaker of "the mother," recalling the children her abortions deprived her of, and the figure in "What shall I give my children who are poor?" lamenting her inability to give her children access to rich life. Other mothers include the tough one in Betty Gates's "Mamma Settles the Dropout Problem":

> Umgoing up side yo head
> Wit my big fiss
> An' when I swings
> I don aim to miss[7]

and the boldly eccentric mother in Lucille Clifton's "Admonitions":

```
children
when they ask you
why is your mama so funny
say
she is a poet
she don't have no sense.⁸
```

Often, as in poems like Sterling Brown's "When the Saints Go Ma'chin In" and Owen Dodson's "Black Mother Praying," a poet combines mother and religion to express deep emotion. This is effective because both are still points in the turning world of black experience both in Africa and in the diaspora, so combining them provides emotional resonance.

Afro-American attitudes toward mother are extremely complex, but in almost all the mother poems, mother is above criticism, the almost perfect symbol of black struggle, suffering, and endurance. Reading about her, we know where Sterling Brown's strong men come from, for she says:

```
You must keep going
You can't stop there; World will
waive; will be
facetious, angry. You can't stop there
You have to keep on going.⁹
```

Black women singers are our culture heroes. More durable than movie stars, the giants among them endure and symbolize both transcendent beauty and deeply experienced pain. The images of black women singers alternate between expressing what they share with other black people and what makes them extraordinary. The African proverb says, "The spirit will not descend without a song,"¹⁰ and black women singers (there is no comparable body of poems by male singers) express, manage, modulate the pain we sustain. Treatment of this subject goes back as far as Dunbar's "When Malindy Sings" and comes right up to Don Lee's dedication in *We Walk the Way of the New World:* "To those who helped create a New Consciousness ... Miriam Makeba, Nina Simone: two internationally known black women entertainers that are consistently black and relevant, can u name me two brothers/blackmen that are as ..."¹¹

Dunbar establishes the humble Malindy as a symbol by deflecting from details of her appearance and personality and emphasizing her naturalness (as opposed to Miss Lucy's studied art), which is in concord with and even surpasses nature, so that birds are awed by her singing. She is also a bridge, a conduit making the transcendent immanent in the lives of singers. Langston Hughes in "Jazzonia" and Claude McKay in "The Harlem Dancer" illustrate the Negro Renaissance use of black women entertainers. The significance is apparent in three lines of McKay's poem:

> Grown lovelier for passing through a storm
> . . . . . . . . . . . . . . . . . . . . . . . . . . . . . . . .
> But looking at her falsely-smiling face,
> I knew her self was not in that strange place.[12]

Two all-important poems about black women singers are "Ma Rainey" and "Poem to Aretha." The first contrasts Ma Rainey's little and low appearance with her ability to articulate her listeners' experience. Sterling Brown stresses the nexus of shared life between the singer, a priestess, and those she sings for:

> O Ma Rainey
> Sing yo' song;
> Now you's back
> Whah you belong,
> Git way inside us,
> Keep us strong . . .
> O Ma Rainey
> Li'l and low;
> Sing us 'bout de hard luck
> Round our do';
> Sing us 'bout de lonesome road
> We mus' go . . .
>
> Dere wasn't much more de fellow say:
> She jes' gits hold of us dataway.[13]

Another important poem about a woman singer begins linking the singing Aretha to mother images, moves through the pedestrian in her life, refers back to Dinah Washington and Billie Holiday; then Giovanni gives Aretha a scepter of blackness making her the impetus for steps toward the essence of black life and art:

the blacks songs started coming from the singers on stage and the dancers
   in the streets.

Finally, she ascribes political potential to Aretha's songs:

> aretha was the riot was the leader if she had said "come
> let's do it" it would have been done.[14]

Although very early Afro-American poetry (like Phillis Wheatley's), under the influence of neoclassical models that stressed elegance and formality, shunned self-revelation[15] and cherished the universal rather than the racial, Afro-American poetry is replete with examples of our attempts to translate the beauty of black women into language. In the face of the mass of cultural support for the beauty of white women, black poets move to create the uncreated consciousness of their race. An early poem like Holloway's "Miss Melerlee" pictures a black woman:

> Sof' brown cheek, an' smilin' face,
> An' willowy form chuck full o' grace —
> . . . . . . . . . . . . . . . . . . . . . . .
> Pearly teef, an' shinin' hair,
> An' silky arm so plump and bare![16]

Later Gwendolyn Bennett's "To a Dark Girl" links black women to their historical antecedents by mentioning "old forgotten queens" and suggesting that "something of the shackled slave/sobs in the rhythm of your talk."[17] Langston Hughes also reflects a history-tuned sense of black women in "When Sue Wears Red" with references to "ancient cameo/Turned brown by the ages" and "A queen from some time-dead Egyptian night."[18]

Gwendolyn Brooks, writing before the 1960s black-is-beautiful wave, provides a window on our perverse preoccupation with color, hair, noses, and lips. A woman asks for an upsweep with humpteen baby curls:

> Got Madam C. J. Walker's first
> Got Poro Grower next
> Ain't none of 'em worked with me . . .
> But I ain't vexed
>
> Long hair's out of style anyhow, ain't it?[19]

In "the ballad of chocolate Mabbie," a seven-year-old girl's boy friend prefers "a lemon-hued lynx/with sand-waves loving her brow."[20] Annie Allen's husband takes up with a "maple banshee" and thinks of his wife:

> Not that woman! (Not that room!
> Not that dusted demi-gloom!)
> Nothing limpid, nothing meek,
> But a gorgeous and gold shriek.[21]

And, in an extremely unusual poem, Pearl Mae Lee sings a crazed song after her lover is lynched for making love with a white woman who cries rape to cover her acquiescence:

> At school, your girls were the bright little girls.
> You couldn't abide dark meat.
> Yellow was for to look at
> Black for the famished to eat . . .
>
> You grew up with bright skins on the brain
> And me in your black folks' bed.[22]

Contemporary Afro-American poetry often glories in details of black beauty. Ishmael Reed mentions "juicy Ethiopian art/Lips,"[23] Michael Harper uses "nutmeg reflection"[24] and "raisin skin."[25] Emmett Till's mother's face has the "tint of pulled taffy."[26] Mrs. Sallie Smith is a "low-brown butterball,"[27] Dougherty Long has a gingerbread mama "all sweet and brown" valued above collard greens, candied yams, and new watermelon.[28] Black breasts against a windowpane are blackbirds for Lucille Clifton;[29] Carolyn Rodgers refers to ashy skin and nappy hair;[30] Dudley Randall likens lips to cherries in their curve, grapes in their fullness, and blackberries in their sweetness.[31] Hoagland starts with "honeystain," compares breasts to "african gourds" and "american pumpkins," and calls his woman "night interpreted";[32] and he pulls out all stops in the rash of food imagery in "love Child—a black aesthetic": "sweet baked apple dappled cinnamon speckled," "nutmeg freckled peach brandy and amber wine woman," african pepper pot, coffee flowing with cream, brown sugar, cocoa, candied yams, sweet-potato pie, raisins, blackberry pie, and honey love syrup.[33]

Note that the audience for black poetry has historically been white and distanced from black standards, and the poetry reflects that in the shift from the general descriptions of early poetry to the specificity of the poetry, for a changed audience, for the 1960s and 1970s. Also, black women can look so many different ways, there is so much intraracial variation, that poetry cannot show an "ideal." Finally, much recent poetry, despite the interest in the physical represented by black-is-beautiful, considers moral, intellectual, and political stances more critical than physical beauty.

In 1918, when William Stanley Braithwaite wrote an introduction to Georgia Douglas Johnson's *The Heart of a Woman*, he emphasized the short time (less than fifty years) that women had spoken or acted with a sense of freedom; he went on to say:

Sadness is a kind of felicity with woman, paradoxical as it may seem; and it is so because through this inexplicable felicity *they* touched, intuitionally caress reality . . . Mrs. Johnson creates just that reality of woman's heart and experience with astonishing raptures. It is a kind of privilege to know so much about the secrets of woman's nature, a privilege all the more to be cherished when given, as in these poems, with exquisite utterance, with such lyric sensibility.[34]

Du Bois wrote the foreword to Johnson's 1922 *Bronze.* He starts by mentioning her blackness, which Braithwaite had omitted and which the poet herself had downplayed in her earlier volume. "Her work is simple, sometimes trite, but it is singularly sincere and true, and as a revelation of the soul struggle of the women of a race, it is invaluable."[35] In his 1970 introduction to June Jordan's *Some Changes,* Julius Lester wrote:

June Jordan is a black poet, a black woman poet. That's a devastating combination. To be black and to be a woman. To be a double outsider, to be twice oppressed, to be more than invisible. That's a triple vision. June Jordan is faithful to the three primary aspects of her being.[36]

In recent years the image of black women in Afro-American poetry has become more autobiographical (more in keeping with the assertive mood of the race than with the confessional trends in Euro-American poetry). It is as if the younger women poets see themselves as similes of their sisters. Poems in this category include Mari Evans's "To Mother and Steve" with its search for love and struggle against the thrall of drugs. Her "into blackness softly" is like both Audre Lorde's "Naturally" and Johari Amini's "Identity (For Don L. Lee)" in registering the poet's new black consciousness. Carolyn Rodger's "Me, In Kulu Se & Karma" is autobiographical, as is Nikki Giovanni's "Nikki-Rosa." Sonia Sanchez's "poem for my father," "poem for etheridge," and "why I don't get high on shit" are all autobiographical, and the whole section "In these Dissenting . . . Surrounding Ground and Autobiography" in *Revolutionary Petunias* is autobiographical.

White women are, as part of their new consciousness, fighting stereotypes. No student of this movement, I use Mary Ellmann's categories (formlessness, passivity, instability, confinement, piety, materiality, spirituality, irrationality, compliancy, the shrew, and the witch)[37] as a gauge. Few of these seem appropriate to Afro-American images of black women because they are rarely seen as weak or frivolous or incompetent. As Faulkner said of Dilsey, black women in Afro-American poetry have "endured." They have had, given their economic and political powerlessness, and their social status, no other choice. Passivity, for example, is inapplicable. Except for examples like Emmett Till's mother (but it may just be that we cannot see the "chaos" in her "red prairie"),[38] the women are action-oriented: aggressiveness is part of the matriarch stereotype black women labor under. Passivity had a certain vogue under the 1960s influence of Muslim ideology, which elevated black men—often at the expense of black women:

> blackwoman:
> is an
> in and out
> rightsideup
> action-image
> of her man . . .
> in other
> (blacker) words:
> she's together
> if
> he
> bes[39]

though Kay Lindsey says:

> . . . But now that the revolution needs numbers
> Mothers got a new position
> Five steps behind manhood.
>
> And I thought sittin' in the back of the bus
> Went out with Martin Luther King.[40]

All the examples of irrationality I found in my survey of Afro-American poetry were in the blues tradition of loving a man who doesn't love you; but who *does* love wisely? Compliancy doesn't apply: black women are not portrayed as compliant to their men, their children, or their white employers. Ellman's spirituality means refining or ennobling the man who loves one;[41] for black women it means strengthening, centering black men, being keepers of the flame of black culture (as seen in the coalescence of women and the integrity of Africa in the poetry of the 1960s).

Molly Means, "Chile of the devil, the dark, and witch,"[42] who changes a young bride into a howling dog, is the only explicit witch my research revealed—though Saint Louis woman, who enchants a man with diamond rings, power, and store-bought hair,[43] is perhaps an urbane, urban witch.

The most common stereotypes of black women are tragic mulatto, hot-blooded exotic whore, and matriarch.[44] I found no examples of tragic mulatto in the poetry. I found several street women (Gwendolyn Brooks's Sadie, Countee Cullen's "Black Magdelens," and Fenton Johnson's "The Scarlet Woman"), but none of them were exotic. Sapphire is another stereotype in black life, but she is nowhere visible in formal Afro-American poetry, where the relations between black women and black men are usually tender, desperate, or tragic, but never angry, domineering or aggressive. The strong black mammy, "bad-talking, ball-busting, strong enough to sustain her family and herself through the hardest conditions,"[45] does exist in the literature, but she is humanized by being scaled down as Gwendolyn Brooks does Mrs. Sallie Smith, Emmett Till's mother, Mrs. Small, and Big Bessie, who "throws" her son into the street. Washington says:

> To outsiders, she is the one-dimensional Rock of Gibraltar—strong of back, long of arm, invincible. But to those writers whose perceptions are shaped by their own black womanhood, who can take us into the dark recesses of the soul, she is an individual—profound, tragic, mysterious, sacred, and unfathomable—strong in many ways, but not all.[46]

While this may be true of fiction, few of the images in Afro-American poetry reveal the complexity she describes.

The epic (heroic, archetypal) is an aspect of many of the images of black women in Afro-American poetry, though few poems, and most of them are recent, have only this thread:

> and the breath of your life
> sustains us . . .
> the female in the middle passage,
> you endure
> we endured through you[47]

and

> i am a blk/woo OOMAN
> my face
>          my brown
>          bamboo/colored
> black/berry/face
> will spread itself over
> this western hemisphere and
> be remembered
>          be sunnnnnNNGG
> for i will be called
>          QUEEN
> walk/move in

blk/queenly ways.
and the world
    shaken by
by blkness
    will channnnnNNGGGEEE
colors. and be
    reborn.
        blk. again.[48]

and


            I
            am a black woman
            tall as a cypress
            strong
            beyond all definition still
            defying place
            and time
            and circumstance
                assailed
                    impervious
                        indestructible
            Look
                on me and be
            renewed.[49]

Usually, however, the heroic is a strand in a poem about a mother or a singer. Consider Helene Johnson's "The Mother's Rock" or Imamu Baraka's "leroy," where the mother is seen as the transmitter and interpreter of "our life from our ancestors/and knowledge, and the strong nigger feeling," with Baraka picturing his mother with "black angels straining above her head,"[50] a bridge between old and new blues. Mari Evans handles the epic this way:


            and the old women gathered
            and sang His praises
            standing
            resolutely together
            like supply sergeants who
            have seen
            everything
            and are still
            Regular Army: It
            was fierce and
            not melodic and
            although we ran
            the sound of it
            stayed in our ears . . .[51]

Robert Hayden's "Runagate, Runagate" provides a magnificent example of the epic black woman:

> Rises from their anguish and their power,
>
> Harriet Tubman
>
> woman of earth, whipscarred,
> a summoning, a shining
>
> Mean to be free
> . . . . . . . . . . . . . . . . . . . . . . . . . . . . .
> and fear starts a-murbling, Never make it,
> we'll never make it. *Hush that now,*
> and she's turned upon us, levelled pistol
> glinting in the moonlight;
> Dead folks can't jaybird-talk, she says;
> you keep on going now or die, she says.
>
> Wanted . . . Harriet Tubman     alias The General
> alias Moses     Stealer of Slaves
>
> In league with Garrison     Alcott     Emerson
> Garrett     Douglass     Thoreau     John Brown
>
> Armed and known to be Dangerous
>
> Wanted     Reward     Dead or Alive
> . . . . . . . . . . . . . . . . . . . . . . . . . . . . .
> Mean mean mean to be free.[52]

Images of black women in Afro-American poetry come very close to what Ellison said about the blues: "Their attraction lies in this, that they at once express the agony of life and the possibility of conquering it through sheer toughness of spirit."[53] The limitation is that the intensely symbolic nature of the images has often limited both the range of women we see and the ways in which they are presented. We need, now, poems to reflect our myriad realities.

# PART TWO

## THREE ACTIVISTS IN FOCUS

# SHARON HARLEY

# 7

## ANNA J. COOPER:
## A VOICE FOR BLACK WOMEN

On August 10, 1859, eleven years after the official declaration of the women's rights movement in the United States was issued at the Seneca Falls Conference, Anna J. Cooper was born, in Raleigh, North Carolina. She was the daughter of Hannah Stanley, a slave, and George Washington Haywood, Hannah's master. Some people believed Anna's father was a slave, but Anna wrote that her father was her mother's master, although her mother "was always too modest and shame-faced to mention him."[1]

At a very early age, Anna exhibited unusual intellectual capacity. By the time she was nine, she began serving as a "pupil-teacher" at Saint Augustine's Normal and Collegiate Institute. While at Saint Augustine's, Anna met the Reverend George A. C. Cooper, an Episcopal priest, whom she married in 1877. After only two years of marriage, Anna Cooper became a widow.[2]

After the death of her husband, Anna entered Oberlin College, which admitted blacks prior to the Civil War. She received a bachelor of arts degree with honors in 1884 and a honorary master's degree in 1887.[3] Leonard Garver, one of her classmates in the 1884 graduation class, predicted Anna's future in a letter to her:

> Thine is a wealth of womanhood:
> A mind of might: a heart of good.
> We feel that in the future thine
> A mission is almost divine.[4]

Although American historiography regarding the women's rights movement has tended to exclude the efforts of black females, beginning

in the late nineteenth century and continuing throughout her long lifetime, Anna Julia Cooper wrote numerous articles, books, and pamphlets
mainly about the importance of improving the status of black women
and about the benefits an improved status in society would bring to the
black race. Although few women in the nineteenth century had their ideas
about the rights of women published, Cooper did in 1892—an excellent
book entitled *A Voice from the South, By a Black Woman of the South.*
In this work she discussed the lowly status of black women in the United
States, and how important the black woman was in uplifting the entire
black race. She may have been inspired to publish her views by the earlier
publication of a work on black women by another Washington, D.C.,
resident. Reverend Alexander Crummell, pastor of Saint Luke's Protestant
Episcopal Church, sold over 500,000 copies of his book *The Black Woman
of the South: Her Neglects and Her Needs* to raise money for a home
for black women in the District of Columbia.[5]

Anna J. Cooper was not concerned with merely narrating the
experiences of black women in her book; she was also advancing the
idea that black women need to speak up for themselves and not allow
black men always to speak for them. As she exclaimed in the opening
pages of her work,

Our Caucasian barristers are not to blame if they cannot quite put themselves in the dark man's place, neither should the dark man be wholly
expected, fully and adequately to reproduce the exact voice of the Black
woman.[6]

Her reference to black males was not an attempt to indict them but an
expression of her belief that no one else could "more accurately tell
the weight and fret of the long dull pain than the open-eyed but hitherto
voiceless black woman of America."[7] Her book was intended for the eyes
of black males as well as females, since the former were partially to blame
for the low status of women. She spoke and wanted other black women
to speak about their true position in society so that a clearer and more
accurate picture of their real status would be known.

In promoting the cause of women's rights, Cooper's major concern was
to see that higher education was made more readily available to black
women. She held that whenever women sought higher education or had
aspirations to higher goals in life, they were usually discouraged by those
who considered these attainments to be solely male prerogatives. Cooper
believed that most women had no real goals of their own or desire for
education, since they thought that their only value was to please men.
Thus, it was not surprising to Cooper that the average woman gloried
in her ignorance.

**Anna Julia Cooper**

Cooper discovered that the reasons why education was not encouraged among women ranged from the belief that it interfered with marriage to the idea that it

was incompatible with the shape of the female cerebrum, and that even if it could be acquired it must inevitably unsex women destroying the lisping, clinging, tenderly helpless, and beautifully dependent creatures whom men would so heroically think for and so gallantly fight for.[8]

Cooper admitted that while these ideas were more prevalent in the eighteenth century, there were still men and even some women who held similar beliefs in the late nineteenth century. The men who still held such views about women suffered from a myopic view of females and their contributions to society.

Cooper believed that some educated black men, too, held negative views of women, and she partially blamed them for not encouraging women in educational endeavors and for not making themselves aware of the depressed conditions of women, although they were aware of other developments in the world. She therefore maintained that the principal issue in the relation between the sexes was no longer a question of how women could stifle their growth and ignore their interests in order to make themselves more acceptable to men, but how men could adjust to the demands of women.

Her pleas for higher education for women were not based solely on her personal experiences, for in her research on the educational attainments of women, she had found that there had been only a few black females on college campuses during the period from 1886 to 1889; for example, during this period there were only seventeen at Fisk University and five at Oberlin College.[9] These figures and her own personal experiences caused her to question the worth of a society that did not encourage its female population to achieve, both within and outside the home.

Cooper saw little hope for any civilization which ignored its women, especially their important role in the home. Her association of females with the home may appear contradictory to the goal of improving the status of black women. In a Victorian vein, not unlike her white female counterparts, she felt that elevating the black woman's position in society would uplift the entire black race, since it was the woman who influenced the man "by directing the earliest impulses of his character" as a child.[10] An educated woman with broad interests, a woman who was respected and considered to have worth, could better train young black children—the future generation of the race—as well as have influence outside of the home. She maintained that black male leaders who were attempting to improve the condition of the race exclusive of the black female should realize that all such attempts would "prove abortive unless so directed as to utilize the indispensable agency of an elevated and trained womanhood."[11] In an effort to make more and more black males aware of the importance of women to the regeneration and the progress of the race, she read a paper on this subject before the 1886 Convocation of Colored Clergy of the Protestant Episcopal Church in Washington. The availability of education to women would enable them to reason and express themselves and would provide them with the "training and stimulus which would enable and encourage women to administer to the world the bread it needs as well as the sugar it cries for,"[12] Cooper declared.

As she observed, the opportunities available to black females in politics were even more limited than those in higher education. Women as a political force were almost nonexistent. Because she felt that black women were truer to the principles of the black race than some black males—who for various reasons seemed to forsake the cause of the race—Cooper maintained that a woman should be in the forefront of the fight for black rights. The black woman, she asserted, "is always sound . . . and orthodox on questions affecting the well-being of the race, and . . . you do not find [her] selling her birthright for a mess of pottage."[13] It is doubtful whether blacks of either sex could have truly represented black interests at a time when white supremacy reigned.

Although she criticized black males for not always being true to the race and for not supporting the endeavors of women, Cooper was by no means antimale. She dedicated her most noted work on black women, *A Voice from the South,* to Bishop Benjamin Arnett, whom she highly respected for his dedication to female causes and to any other causes that needed his help. Moreover, in her publication on the Grimké family, she poetically expressed her deep admiration for Dr. Francis J. Grimké, pastor of the Fifteenth Street Presbyterian Church, as follows:

> His Work is done;
> He sat a while at eventide
> To watch his sun go down
> And think upon
> His fruitful years and noble pride,
> His silvered hair his crown.[14]

Although critical of black males on occasion, Cooper, like many black females, nevertheless considered the struggle of women as part of the overall black struggle.

Cooper realized that the difference in circumstances of black women as juxtaposed to those of white women tended to force the two groups to differ in their emphasis and focus in their respective women's rights groups. The sufferings of black women were far worse than those of white women because the former were discriminated against as a result of their race as well as their sex. Due to the commonality of their experiences in the United States, black women shared a sense of affliction with black men which white females did not necessarily share with white males. She described a clear example of this discrimination toward all blacks regardless of their sex when she reported that while in a train station she was perplexed about which rest room she and other black females were supposed to use—the one with the sign "For Ladies" or the other rest room "For Colored People."[15] Thus, it would have been absurd for black women totally to divorce their struggles from those of the black male, in light of the attitude held toward them by most whites, male or female.

In analyzing the relationship between black males and black females, Anna J. Cooper clearly saw that both groups were victims of centuries of degradation and oppression designed to keep them apart. In an untitled poem she succinctly expressed their common position in American society:

> For woman's cause is man's, they rise or sink
> Together, dwarfed or godlike, bond or free.[16]

Whereas white feminists may have been able to afford the luxury of devoting all of their energies to women's rights movements, black female activists were forced to fight not only for women's rights but for the rights of all blacks. A section of her work on women was devoted to a discussion of race prejudice, as were some of her articles, speeches, and other manuscripts. Like Anna Cooper, other black females, including Ida B. Wells-Barnett and Mary Church Terrell, voiced their opposition to the lynching of blacks, which was rampant during the period from 1890 to 1920. This criminal destruction of blacks further heightened the racial consciousness of black females as well as black males.

A charter member of the Colored Women's League of Washington (founded 1892), Cooper attended a number of women's meetings. She was present at the first National Conference of Colored Women in Boston in 1895.[17] Despite her involvement in the Women's League and other organizations, Cooper held that "the solution of our problem will be individual and not en masse."[18] Her statement appears to reflect a degree of naïveté considering the late-nineteenth-century increase in Jim Crowism, which forced members of the black community to unite for self-help and racial advancement. But the statement may have been a reaction to the constant joining of clubs and organizations engaged in by some members of the Washington black community. Her opinion of this aspect of the Washington black scene was supported by members of the Federal Writers Project in their study of Washington, D.C.; they wrote "Washington Negroes are great 'joiners.'"[19]

An integral element of Cooper's fight for women's rights and the elevation of the entire black race was her commitment to the education of black youth. During her long teaching career in various cities in the United States, Anna J. Cooper waged a continuous battle to improve the educational conditions of both black youths and adults, especially in Washington, D.C. Prior to entering the District of Columbia school system, Cooper taught at the Oberlin Academy, Wilberforce University, and Saint Augustine's College. In 1887, she moved to Washington to begin a teaching career that extended over forty years at the "M" Street High School (later Dunbar High School). From 1901 to 1906, she served as principal, the second black female principal in the school's history.[20] In 1905, she was accused of disloyalty for refusing to use the prescribed inferior textbooks and curriculum for black students, which had been proposed by Congress "to give the pupils of this school [Dunbar] a course of study commensurate with their alleged inferior abilities."[21] She was adamant in her insistence that Dunbar students have the same choice of subjects as the students in the white schools of the District. As a result of the backing of a large segment of the black community and the general recognition of her outstanding ability, the charges of insubordination were dropped.[22]

As principal of Dunbar, Cooper was able to obtain from such prestigious colleges as Brown, Yale, and Harvard a promise to admit qualified black students from Dunbar. She personally aided students who were able to pass entrance examinations at these schools with honors. Believing that segregated education had a negative effect on black youth, she worked diligently to get black students admitted to top colleges. She opposed Booker T. Washington's emphasis on vocational training for black youth, because she felt that all students should have the opportunity to pursue academic courses.[23]

Despite (or perhaps because of) her efforts on behalf of black youth, Cooper was "not rehired" as principal during the 1906 reshuffling of teachers and administrators within the school system. She was left without a job. Although the failure of Cooper to be rehired by the school board, which at this time included its first black female, Mary Church Terrell, may be attributable to the fact that many individuals objected to having a female principal, a more likely explanation is that she was being punished for her opposition to white superiority by refusing to use inferior curriculum and textbooks for students of "M" Street High School. In conjunction with several other teachers who had been dismissed, Cooper sent a letter to the Board of Education demanding that she be reinstated.[24]

Referring to this incident in a letter to her classmates at Oberlin, Cooper wrote: "The dominant forces of our country are not yet tolerant of the higher steps for colored youth, so that while our course of study was for the first time being saved, my head was lost in the fray, and I moved west."[25] While fighting for her reappointment to the school system, Cooper served as chairperson of the Department of Languages at Lincoln Institute in Jefferson City, Missouri. In September of 1910, Dr. W. A. Davidson, the newly appointed head of the Washington School System, had Cooper reappointed as a Latin teacher, but not as principal.[26]

Her fight to be rehired was only one of many battles which she waged as a teacher in the Washington school system. In an effort to improve her classification in the school system, Cooper applied for the "Group B" salary reserved for the "superior teachers." According to the Board of Education, her application was denied because she failed to score high enough on the exam. Not willing to accept the board's decision, Cooper took the matter to the Complaints and Appeals Commission, which refused to hear her case, pointing to the low score on her exam.[27]

Cooper was assisted in her fight for a promotion by Mrs. N. Stone Scott, her former classmate at Oberlin College. Describing her as "one of the foremost colored women of the generation," Mrs. Scott wrote a letter to the wife of President Calvin Coolidge concerning Anna's failure to obtain the "Group B" salary.[28] To Anna Cooper, the major consideration of the Board of Education in the granting of higher salaries was not examination scores, but the color of the applicant. As she wrote in a letter to a friend,

I had the hardihood to point out the enormous discrepancy in the proportion of those "superior" salaries in the white and colored schools at which time only two out of fifty-six were in our schools, although the colored population comprised one-third of the total enrollment.[29]

Cooper was just as active outside of the school setting as within. She was a member of the NAACP, the National Association of Educators, a life member of the Phillis Wheatley branch of the Young Women's Christian Association; in addition, she was a special organizer of the YWCA girls clubs from 1911 to 1915 and a supervisor of the Colored Social Settlement in Southwest Washington.[30] Although much attention has been given to the speaking engagements of another Washington black woman, Mary Church Terrell, Cooper was also often in demand as a speaker. In September 1902 she presented a paper entitled "The Ethics of the Negro" at the Biennial Session of Friends' General Conference in Asbury Park, New Jersey. In this address as well as in others, Cooper advised blacks to have a clear idea of their goals in life, for she asserted that "where there is no vision, the people perish."[31]

In 1900, Anna Julia Cooper traveled to Europe, where she spoke before the Pan-African Conference in London,[32] organized by the West Indian barrister and Pan-Africanist Henry Sylvester Williams and attended by the later noted Pan-Africanist W. E. B. Du Bois. Twenty-nine years later, Cooper wrote to Du Bois, requesting that he reply to Claude Bowers's negative depiction of blacks in the Reconstruction governments: "It seems to me that *The Tragic Era* should be answered—adequately, fully ably, finally and again it seems to me that Thou are the man!"[33] The subsequent publication of W. E. B. Du Bois's *Black Reconstruction* attempted to refute the false allegations made in Bowers's work about black politicians of the Reconstruction period.

In addition to her activities on behalf of Pan-Africanism, women's rights, education for black youth, and racial equality, Cooper, childless herself, raised her five adopted nieces and nephews. In order to provide adequate facilities for her enlarged family, she purchased the home of General LeFevre, a retired member of Congress. In deference to the difficulties that blacks in segregated Washington had in finding decent housing, Cooper thanked General LeFevre for selling his LeDroit Park home, where blacks in the past had been excluded except as servants.[34]

In addition to teaching, raising a family, and civic work, Anna J. Cooper found time to pursue her own academic endeavors. In 1925, at the age of sixty-five, she took a leave of absence from the "M" Street High School in order to complete the work on a doctorate in Latin at the Sorbonne which she had begun at Columbia University.[35] In December of that year, she was honored at a ceremony at the Rankin Chapel of Howard University sponsored by the Alpha Kappa Alpha sorority and addressed by Dr. Alain Locke. In responding to Locke's words of praise and on receiving her degree, Cooper declared: "I take at your hands, . . . this diploma, not as a symbol of cold intellectual success on my achievements at the Sorbonne, but with warm pulsing heart throbs of a people's satisfaction in my humble endeavors to serve them."[36] Although the number of black female Ph.D.s was small, Dr. Cooper considered her accomplishments examples of what most black women could achieve if given the chance.

In a *Washington Post* article, Dr. Cooper was described as an unusual woman, because she was such a highly educated black woman.[37] Although this was true, it was not because she possessed intellectual abilities other black women did not have. There were a number of highly educated black women on the faculty of Dunbar Senior High School and Howard University; but most black women did not have the opportunity to pursue a formal education, and therefore they were unable to cultivate their intellectual abilities. This was one of the reasons why Cooper struggled to see that all women as well as men would have an opportunity to better themselves through obtaining higher education. She wanted women to fight for higher education and for black men to fight with them—or at least offer some encouragement.

After retiring from the District of Columbia school system, Cooper continued to struggle for the advancement of the race, especially in the area of education. She devoted her later years to the education of black adults. In 1930 she became president of Frelinghuysen University of Employed Colored Persons, an institution founded in 1906 by Jesse Lawson. Although Cooper was more inclined to support the Du Bois philosophy of education than that of Booker T. Washington, she was aware of the need to improve the vocational skills of the masses of black Washingtonians; thus the school offered both vocational and academic courses. She graciously lent the "university" the use of her home at 201 "T" Street, N.W., when it became necessary to have a permanent location. She subsequently issued a pamphlet calling for accreditation of the institution and for racial equality.[38]

Believing that "we should do things for ourselves," she felt a strong sense of pride in the "university" and in other black enterprises. Since the 1890s, blacks had formed and supported large numbers of self-help agencies, social organizations, and schools. Even the moderate Carter G. Woodson, founder of the Association for the Study of Negro Life and History ("Negro" changed in 1972 to "Afro-American"), favored the formation of separate black organizations.[39] Despite her conscientious efforts, Frelinghuysen University was never accredited, however, and faded out of existence in the 1950s.[40]

Besides the scholarly discussion of the situation of blacks, Cooper felt that it was also essential to actively work to improve the conditions of the less influential members of the black race. In reference to her efforts on behalf of impoverished black people, Charles Weller, the executive director of the Associated Charities of the District of Columbia, stated:

Altogether, in a city where there were a large number of cultured, resourceful, public spirited colored people, Mrs. Cooper, proved herself to be one of the most helpful workers for the intelligent advancement of the best interests of less fortunate colored people.[41]

Cooper's involvement in a number of activities was based upon her conviction that "it isn't what we say about ourselves, it's what our lives stand for."[42] Anna Julia Cooper stood for education and service, and was thus an inspiration to black women to

live and learn and be all that not harms distinctive womanhood. For woman is not underdeveloped man but diverse.[43]

In her autobiography, *The Third Step,* Anna Cooper described the principles that guided her throughout her long lifetime. In February of 1964, at the age of 104, Anna J. Cooper, a noted black female educator and fighter for women's rights and for the progress of the black race, passed away in Washington, D.C.[44] In terms of her education, her awareness of issues affecting blacks and her willingness to actively work to advance the causes of the black race, especially those affecting the black woman, she exemplified the finest attributes of black womanhood.

# EVELYN BROOKS BARNETT

# 8

## NANNIE BURROUGHS AND THE EDUCATION
## OF BLACK WOMEN

With the entrenchment of a Jim Crow national policy by the turn of
the twentieth century, black Americans had become increasingly supportive of self-help institutions. Faced with the prospect of "mis-
education" or usually no education in public schools and universities, the
black community accepted the challenge of establishing and/or sustaining
both industrial schools to prepare the race for practical work and institutions of higher learning to produce race leadership, i.e., what Du Bois
termed "The Talented Tenth."[1] The story of this struggle to uplift
the masses is too often confined to white charitable and philanthropic
efforts like the American Missionary Association, the American Baptist
Home Mission Society, and the Phelps-Stokes, Slater, and Rosenwald
funds, rather than to the activities of blacks themselves. However, in
1911 at the Sixteenth Annual Atlanta University Conference, the following significant facts were revealed: from 1885 to 1900 the African
Methodist Episcopal Church raised $1,140,013.31 for schools, while the
A.M.E. Zion Church raised $71,585.21 for this purpose; black Baptists
supported sixty-one schools in 1906; black residents of Virginia annually
contributed from $5,000 to $8,000 for education, while those of Macon
County, Alabama, provided $4,000 for school supplements during 1910
and 1911; and blacks throughout the South annually contributed thousands
of dollars in addition to regular public school funds.

Furthermore, whereas the leadership and contributions of black men
like Booker T. Washington, W. E. B. Du Bois, Joseph C. Price, John Hope,
and Kelly Miller are commonly known, Mary McCleod Bethune is perhaps
the only woman identified by most history texts as having played a
significant role in the building of a black educational institution. The

purpose of this paper, therefore, will be to highlight the important yet overlooked contribution of black women builders of schools by focusing on the work and ideas of Nannie Helen Burroughs as exemplifying early twentieth-century efforts to uplift black women.

In many ways Burroughs's efforts to establish a school for girls went hand in hand with her activities within the organized movement of black Baptist women. In 1900 in Richmond, at the Twentieth Annual Session of the National Baptist Convention, the Reverend L. G. Jordan, corresponding secretary of the Foreign Mission Board, recommended the formation of a Baptist women's convention, which would serve as an adjunct to the men's convention and labor particularly in the fields of missionary work. Having been accepted by the men, the motion allowed the women present at this conference to inaugurate the Woman's Auxiliary to the National Baptist Convention. It was within this newly created body that the idea of developing a trade school for girls was formally introduced by Burroughs.[2]

In 1901 at the first annual conference of the Woman's Auxiliary, Nannie Burroughs, having been elected corresponding secretary at the Richmond meeting, proposed "that a special committee be appointed to advise with our Board to devise plans for the beginning of the Training School, this committee to report at our next annual session."[3] By the time of the Seventh Annual Conference of the Woman's Auxiliary, Burroughs's dream was quickly becoming a reality. The school was to be called the National Baptist Training School for Women and Girls and would produce missionaries, Sunday school teachers, stenographers, bookkeepers, musicians, cooks, laundresses, housemaids, and other skilled workers. Despite the history of the National Baptist Convention in support of black education, the men did not immediately endorse a school for girls. Criticism focused primarily on its training women to be workers and breadwinners, rather than missionaries exclusively. By the 1905 convention, however, the men had become more amenable to this idea and recorded that "each succeeding year has given greater emphasis to the importance of having trained women in the race, if we are to have our share of skilled labor which will ever remain the basis of real progress in a material way."[4]

Settling upon Washington as the location for the school, a committee of seven was formed to find the most suitable site and afterward to incorporate. However, at the meeting in Washington in 1907 at the Nineteenth Street Baptist Church, only Nannie Burroughs and two others were present. Depositing $1,000 as down payment toward the $6,000 total, they secured a six-acre tract of land in a section of the city known as Lincoln Heights, upon which were located a four-story frame house,

**Nannie Helen Burroughs**

a well, several fruit trees, a large stable, and a barn. The committee of three then proceeded to incorporate, deeding the certificate of title to the training school committee while naming the institution the National Training School for Women and Girls. Omitting the word "Baptist" from the original title was probably Burroughs's idea, since she had conceived of the school as serving women of all faiths. Also initially chartering the school independent of the control of the Baptist Convention could have possibly been a conscious effort on her part. She was known to publicly criticize the Baptist men for fighting among themselves. In fact, the board of trustees for the school was structured in such a way as to constitute a membership of eighty, all black and mostly women.[5]

These actions on her part eventually alienated certain factions of the men's convention. Although many individual ministers remained loyal and outstanding supporters of the school, a donation to the school was never given in the name of the National Baptist Convention. From 1920 to 1938 the autonomous leadership of Nannie Burroughs was a matter of controversy, culminating on June 22, 1938, in a resolution adopted by the National Baptist Convention to "withdraw all connections, allegiance, and support from the said training school at Washington, D.C." In 1947 Burroughs and the National Baptist Convention reconciled their differences, with the latter group formally endorsing the school.[6]

The National Training School for Women and Girls officially opened on October 19, 1909, with Nannie Burroughs as president. By the end of the first year the school had enrolled thirty-one students. Twenty-five years later the institution boasted of more than two thousand women trained at the high school and junior college level in fields like missionary work, domestic science, clerical and secretarial skills, farming, and even printing. Housed in the campus dormitory, the girls came from all over the United States as well as from Africa and the Caribbean. Burroughs emphasized the training of spiritual character, and thus the school operated along strict moral codes. The institution was called the School of the Three B's for the importance placed on the Bible, bath, and broom as tools for race advancement.[7]

Yet, the National Training School attempted to speak concretely to the material conditions surrounding black women. American society demanded that the black woman work no less than her man for survival, while for many decades both sexes were for the most part limited either to agricultural work in the South or domestic service in rural and urban areas throughout the nation. During the training school's first year of operation, approximately 54.7 percent of black women ten years of age and over were gainfully employed, as opposed to only 19.6 percent of comparable white women. Although the demand for labor during World

War I eventuated in the Great Migration of blacks out of the South, along with a larger inclusion of black women, as well as men, in northern industry, the "return to normalcy" in the decade following 1920 resulted in massive lay-offs and a sharp decline in job opportunities. By 1930, nine-tenths of all black working women were still in farm or domestic work, the only change being that the majority were now employed in the latter field. In 1930 black people constituted one-third of all workers in domestic service. The vast majority were relegated to the status of household servants, with black women outnumbering black men seven to one in this capacity. Moreover, large numbers of black women labored in other categories of domestic and personal service—laundresses, waitresses, midwives, hair dressers, charwomen, and elevator tenders.[8]

Domestic work offered the black woman a menial, low-paying livelihood—a precarious position unregulated by minimum wage laws, social security benefits, and standard work hours or conditions. Although a minimum wage law of $20.50 per week was enacted in the spring of 1920 covering women working in the hotels and restaurants of Washington, black women enjoyed few of these benefits. Most employers, unable to exploit the cheapest labor on their own terms, displaced black for white women; domestics in private homes were not affected by the bill.[9]

Likewise, in 1929 the federal Minimum Wage Board recommended a wage of $14.50 per week for unskilled labor in laundries—two dollars less than the minimum wage for all other industries. Nannie Burroughs denounced this action, charging the board with racism, inasmuch as black women comprised almost 75 percent of all laundresses at the time. In a letter to Archibald Grimké, president of the Washington branch of the National Association for the Advancement of Colored People, Miss Burroughs wrote: "This piece of class legislation should be repudiated by Public Protest. In former Conferences, it was said a woman could not live decently on $14.50 per week in the District. This law demands 'A Decent living wage!'"[10]

The concentration of black women in household service reflected neither their satisfaction with such employment nor their willingness to accept the drudgery of its work conditions. The general unpopularity of these jobs was evidenced in the extremely high turnover rate for black women. According to Elizabeth Ross Haynes, Domestic Service Secretary of the U.S. Employment Service from 1920 to 1924 and first black woman elected to the YWCA national board, turnover in domestic service was also related to illiteracy and lack of training. With the introduction of labor-saving appliances and other technological advances in domestic living, employers often demanded minimum training for efficiency. Frequently they would hire women on a week trial basis—

reluctant to offer even the hope of job security to the prospective worker, who generally had less than a fifth grade education and was thus unable to benefit from the domestic science courses of the public schools.[11]

Stressing the importance of thorough domestic training at the National Training School for Women and Girls, Nannie Burroughs reasoned that "the Negro girl must be taught the art of home-making as a profession, because 98 per cent of them must keep their own homes without any outside 'help' and, according to present statistics, 58 per cent of the women who work out are cooks, nurse-maids, etc."[12] Such training included courses in homemaking, housekeeping, household administration, management for matrons and directors of school dining rooms and dormitories, interior decorating, laundering, and home nursing. Much of this work was implemented in the model cottage on the school grounds, which also served as a practical training center when various conventions were held there. A business venture which provided income for the school along with vocational skill was the establishment of the Sunshine Laundry, a modern system of washing and dry cleaning.[13]

Burroughs's concern for the black working woman was expressed also through her participation in the club movement among black women during the early decades of the twentieth century. In November 1918 she suggested to Mary B. Talbert, president of the National Association of Colored Women, that a conference was needed to discuss the industrial problems of black women. In response to this call, the group planned a meeting to be held in New York on May 7, 1919, to ascertain the role of women in launching a postwar reconstruction program focusing on practical efforts of uplift.[14]

During the 1920s Burroughs assumed this initiative and organized the National Association of Wage Earners in order to attract public attention to the plight of the black working woman. The group was essentially imbued with bourgeois reformism seeking greater participation of black women within American capitalism. Its national board included Nannie Burroughs as president, along with other women outstanding in the National Association of Colored Women—Mary McCleod Bethune, vice-president; Richmond banker Maggie L. Walker, treasurer; and Mary B. Talbert, chairman of the advisory board.[15] The women concentrated more on forums of public interest than activities of a trade unionist nature. The nine-point program of the organization was nevertheless progressive for the era and advocated the following objectives:

1. To develop and encourage efficient workers.
2. To assist women in finding the kind of work for which they seem best qualified.

3. To elevate the migrant classes of workers and incorporate them permanently in service of some kind.

4. To standardize living conditions.

5. To secure a wage that will enable women to live decently.

6. To assemble the multitude of grievances of employers and employees into a set of common demands and strive, mutually, to adjust them.

7. To enlighten women as to the value of organization.

8. To make and supply appropriate uniforms for working women. This shall be done through a profit sharing enterprise operated by the Association.

9. To influence just legislation affecting women wage earners.[16]

Burroughs was extremely influenced by the puritan work ethic, despite her efforts to organize black women workers. To her, the interests of the capitalist could be reconciled with those of the worker if both were honest with each other. Her explanations of unemployment and the capitalist crisis were derived more from a subjective viewpoint than from any economic understanding of production relations. High unemployment for blacks due to preferential hiring of whites and technological displacement was interpreted largely in terms of inefficiency and lack of dependability. Technological development under capitalism was not examined relative to its lawful role in amassing profit, but rather seen as the conscious action of employers who could now "press buttons and get their work done without having to ruin their perfectly good dispositions worrying with unreliable human beings."[17] Obviously, one can deduce from her reasoning that if blacks were to work at optimum efficiency there would be little need or desire on the part of the capitalist for investing in machinery.

Nonetheless, the fact that women worked and were often the sole heads of households led Burroughs consciously to counterpoise the interests of black women to those of black men. Her outspoken feminist attitudes served as a harbinger of future arguments against male chauvinism. Filled with the moralism and piety characteristic of early twentieth-century rhetoric, she insisted on a glorified womanhood, the equal to men of any race. In her own struggle to uplift the economic status of women, she once demanded of black men: "Stop making slaves and servants of our women. We've got to stop singing—'Everybody works but father.'"[18]

During the depression of the 1930s Burroughs shouldered the problems of the black woman as worker and mother—believing her to be hardest hit by the crisis. Poor and overcrowded housing along with long working hours away from home perpetuated what she considered deplorable conditions in which to raise children. In 1933 Burroughs began plans for a children's department in the National Training School. It would house girls aged eight through twelve in order to alleviate some of the burdens on working mothers.[19]

Even earlier, in arguing the need for the passage of the Nineteenth Amendment, she denounced black men who had compromised the struggle for political equality because of cowardice or for material gain, and she urged her sisters to redeem the race through wise use of the ballot. To Burroughs, the suffrage was not only a weapon to enhance the larger enfranchisement and political power of black people during the period of the legalization of segregation; it was also a defense mechanism protecting women from male dominance and abuse in the courts and in general society.[20]

Burroughs's interest in the conditions of women coincided with that of many early black women educators and leaders of her day. Transcending local issues and concerns, women like Nannie Burroughs, Charlotte Hawkins Brown, Cynthia Lugenia Hope (Mrs. John Hope), Janie Porter Barrett, Mary Church Terrell, Margaret Murray Washington (Mrs. Booker T. Washington), and Mary McCleod Bethune worked closely together on a national basis, diffusing their energies between the National Association for Colored Women, the International Council of Women of the Darker Races, the National Association of Wage Earners, various Republican leagues, and other organizations.

During the first half of the 1920s, a less well known and seemingly short-lived organization, the International Council of Women of the Darker Races, exemplified the commitment of the aforenamed women, along with others, in advancing the serious study of conditions historically confronting their sex and race. By forming local study groups in order to analyze conditions in specific areas, e.g., Africa, Haiti, and India, the women hoped to broaden their own cultural knowledge and also gain recognition for the study of women of color as an accepted field. The implementation of this program at the school level was recorded in 1924 by Janie Porter Barrett, president of the Virginia Industrial School for Colored Girls, in a letter to Margaret Washington. Barrett related that during the month of February teachers at the Virginia School had begun to study the history and customs of Haitian women, and planned to study Chinese women in March, Indian women in April, and African women in May.[21]

The concern of these women for the darker races of the world—the Third World, as it is commonly known today—coincided with the period of European and American imperialism. The growth of international finance capital, as well as its export into areas in Africa, Asia, and the islands culminated in the colonial subjugation of peoples of color throughout most of the world. Although the International Council of Women did not apparently address itself to the issue of national liberation struggles, it nonetheless represented a positive thrust. On the one hand, the women praised the French government for a decision concerning race discrimination, thereby overlooking the exploitive role of France in both Africa and Asia; on the other hand they did reject the legacy of Social Darwinist ideas and advocated racial and national pride as a precursor of self-determination. To the council, education was the paramount determinant to the progress of a people. Consequently, the organization endorsed and supported Adelaid Casely-Hayford, wife of African nationalist Joseph Casely-Hayford and also Vice-President for Africa in the International Council of Women, in her efforts to found and maintain the Girls Vocational School and Teacher Training Centre in Freetown, Sierra Leone.[22]

During August 5–7, 1923, the International Council of Women of the Darker Races held its annual general election and constitutional convention at Burroughs's school. Reevaluating their work over the past year, the women adopted the following resolution, which speaks to the general progressive stance of the group:

Whereas we are organized for mutual international cooperation and sympathetic understanding in every forward movement among women and children of the darker races of the world, for the dissemination of knowledge of peoples of color the world over that there may be a larger appreciation of their history and accomplishments and further that they may have a greater degree of respect for their own achievements and a greater pride in themselves, and . . . we, your committee, regard this as the great need of peoples of color the world over.[23]

Perhaps one of the most outstanding features of the women constituting the International Council was their knowledge and appreciation of Afro-American literature and history. Great respect was given to Carter G. Woodson, Walter White, and others who wrote on subjects related to black life. The members of the study groups of the International Council read their works zealously and discussed them among themselves. Margaret Washington, president of the council, often expressed concern for the schools in both the North and the South, "even our own schools where our children are taught nothing except literature of the Caucasian race."[24] The women challenged educators to advance the teaching of Afro-American history, as can be seen in the following provocative statement of the International Council:

Men like Douglass, Langston, Bruce and Revels; women like Sojourner Truth, Frances Ellen Harper and Harriet Tubman, to say nothing of more recent characters of prominence should be as well known by our youth as men and women of any other race, even if their names do not occur quite so often in print. If we as teachers, do not think to do this who will do it?[25]

A committee on education was appointed by the group (including Nannie Burroughs, Addie Dickerson, and Mary Church Terrell) in order to propose a course of study and textbooks for review by school boards across the country.

There was no more staunch an advocate of racial pride and heritage than Nannie Burroughs. She was a life member of the Association for the Study of Negro Life and History. The proceedings of the Twelfth Annual Meeting of the Association held in Pittsburgh in 1927 indicate that Burroughs shared the platform with noted scholars Carter G. Woodson and Alain Locke on the last day of the convention. Her speech, "The Social Value of Negro History," was recounted in the *Journal of Negro History* as follows: "By a forceful address Miss Nannie H. Burroughs emphasized the duty the Negro owes to himself to learn his own story and the duty the white man owes to himself to learn of the spiritual strivings and achievements of a despised but not an inferior people."[26] At the Fourteenth Annual Meeting of the Association, the Training School girls presented "When Truth Gets a Hearing," a pageant dramatizing the black freedom struggle.[27]

An article in the *Pittsburgh Courier* for June 8, 1929, reported that a course in Afro-American history was mandatory for every student at the National Training School for Women and Girls. Interest in the subject was further engendered through annual oratorical and writing contests based on an aspect of black history.[28]

She also worked ardently with the National Association of Colored Women to memorialize the home of Frederick Douglass in Cedar Hill, Anacostia, in the District of Columbia. The dedication of the Douglass Memorial Home on August 12, 1922, was a testimony to the efforts of women like Burroughs, who served on the trustee board of the Frederick Douglass Memorial and Historical Association.[29]

Her strong feelings of racial pride militated against the Training School's being financed primarily by whites. The American Baptist Home Mission Society, the Emmeline Cushing Estate (administered by black lawyer Archibald Grimké), and the Phelps-Stokes and Slater funds were the most outstanding white contributors. However, Nannie Burroughs prided herself in the fact that her school's existence did not rely solely on these groups. To her, the goal of economic self-reliance was the only guarantee for racial uplift and independence. Nor was her school supported mainly under the aegis of the Baptist Woman's Auxiliary. According to William Pickens, Dean of Morgan College from 1915 to 1920 and field secretary of the NAACP for several years thereafter, the school's income had been largely dependent on the individual, eloquent appeal of Burroughs within the black community. He stated that Washington blacks contributed $481.95 in 1909 and $5,251.21 in 1920, while the Woman's Auxiliary donated only $413.50 at its annual Convention in 1920.[30]

Fund drives were covered by white and black newspapers alike, both holding the work of the National Training School in high esteem. After a fire in 1926, the *Washington Evening Star* featured a campaign to raise $100,000 in order to build a new trades hall. Of the $1,600 contributed as of November 16, 1926, the overwhelming amount was derived from Washington citizens. Carter G. Woodson, founder of the Association for the Study of Negro Life and History, donated $500, while lesser amounts came from scholar Anna J. Cooper, musician Gregoria Fraser Goins, and groups like the Red Cap Porters, United Order of Odd Fellows, Young Ladies Protective League, and the Brownie Club. Of the twenty-four donations reported, only four were church-affiliated—their total contribution being less than $200.[31]

The period 1929 to 1930 was especially difficult, and several black leaders attempted to rally support for the school. The minutes of the Thirtieth Annual Report of the Woman's Convention state that Adam Clayton Powell, Sr., pastor of the Abyssinian Baptist Church in New York and trustee of the school, raised $500 from his congregation in order to pay the tuition of an African girl attending the school. Also in that year, Congressman Oscar De Priest of Chicago delivered the commencement address at the school and "inspired the audience until the people actually threw money at him."[32] In a more desperate drive to keep the school in operation during 1934, Mordecai Johnson, president of Howard University, praised Burroughs for soliciting aid more from her own people than from whites.[33]

Juxtaposed alongside her convictions of self-help and self-reliance was the belief in racial purity—an attitude predicated on pride in heritage rather than the arrogance of racism.[34] In 1915 she lauded the black woman for the moral stamina responsible for "preserving an unmixed race."[35] She rejected black emulation of white standards of beauty and charged her sisters with "colorphobia" if they resorted to hair straighteners and skin bleachers in order to change their appearance. Her feelings of race pride predate even the influence of Marcus Garvey, as is evident in her 1904 article, "Not Color but Character." Here she argued that "what every woman who bleaches and straightens out needs, is not her appearance changed, but her mind."[36] In a 1927 article, "With All Thy

Getting," Burroughs challenged her people to spiritualize American life while at the same time exalting their own skin color. Prophetically she exclaimed: "No race is richer in soul quality and color than the Negro. Some day he will realize it and glorify them. He will popularize black."[37]

Dubbed the female Booker T. Washington by many of her contemporaries, Nannie Burroughs posited a far more militant and uncompromising stand on racial issues than the Sage of Tuskegee. Her views permeated the training school and are especially reflected in the school newspaper, *The Worker*. First published on April 15, 1912, this monthly organ depicted a great deal more than usual campus events. In February 1915, *The Worker* headlined Belgian atrocities in the Congo. The article "What the Belgians Did to the Negro" not only outlined the historical development of European colonialism in Africa, but also exposed the exploitation of African labor as lying at the base. Also significant were the Pan-African sentiments expressed. The unity of race and struggle was articulated, with parallels being made explicitly between the burning of "our villages" in the Congo and the lynching of blacks in America.[38]

In another 1915 article, "Trying to Make Washington Look Like Down Home," the school involved itself in agitation around the issue of racial segregation in the District of Columbia. The position taken had historical import, inasmuch as it clearly delineated the National Training School's stand on the then-debated issue of social equality for blacks. Rather than submit to Jim Crow legislation by accepting seating in the back of the bus, the Washington masses were urged to boycott the buses and ride bicycles or hacks, or use roller skates, if necessary.[39]

Motivated by a strong belief in God, Nannie Burroughs felt that racial equality was an ethical apriorism, a spiritual mandate from heaven. Whereas human failings were responsible for prejudice and discrimination, only a struggle waged on moral terms could assure their defeat. Thus she constantly chastised her race for overindulgence in the material aspects of life. To her, preoccupation with wealth and luxury was endemic to white society and would eventually mark its doom. The black contribution to world culture was to address itself to the spiritual salvation of America.[40]

However, her idealism was not a "pie-in-the-sky" philosophy having no concern for poverty, inadequate education, and other concrete conditions of black life. She continually admonished her people to fight for their rights. She renounced the concept of individualism and often stated that the race must unite in a collective struggle. Her mass orientation did not substitute individual examples of achievement for the realization of group advancement. Nor did she believe in race deliverers.[41] On one occasion she told blacks to use "ballots and dollars" to right racism instead of "wasting time begging the white race for mercy."[42] In support of the Washington chapter of the NAACP, she challenged her people in 1934 to courageously demand an end to lynching, when she proclaimed: "It is no evidence of Christianity to have people mock you and spit on you and defeat the future of your children. It is a mark of cowardice."[43] On another occasion she uttered an even more radical pronouncement, stating that "the Negro must serve notice on the world that he is ready to die for justice."[44] When Harlem exploded in March 1935, with black residents revolting against white businessmen and slum landlords, she did not find cause for blame in the action of her people but rather in American racism. Drawing lessons from the American Revolution and quoting from the Declaration of Independence, Burroughs expounded that blacks had reached their endurance limit as a result of patiently suffering "a long train of abuses."[45]

Finally, Nannie Burroughs and the education of black women during the early decades of the twentieth century must be appreciated within the historical context of the larger black struggle. Her efforts to build a school illustrate the camaraderie and cooperation among black women educators. Through Burroughs's labors and ideas, the voices of women are heard articulating the salient questions of the day. Social equality, the franchise, classical versus industrial education, Africa, and economic uplift were issues as much raised and discussed by Nannie Burroughs and her co-workers, as they were debated by Booker T. Washington, W. E. B. Du Bois, and Kelly Miller.

The life of Nannie Helen Burroughs offers a valuable chapter in the unfolding history of women and blacks. On one side, her overemphasis on internal and spiritual qualities was consistent with the dominant ideas of her era. On the other, her attacks on male chauvinism and racism were seminal to the social activity and shibboleths of the 1960s and 1970s, and thus make her the more unique in terms of her own milieu.

# GERALD R. GILL

# 9

## "WIN OR LOSE-WE WIN": THE 1952 VICE PRESIDENTIAL CAMPAIGN OF CHARLOTTA A. BASS

Since 1968, one has witnessed the increasing emergence of black women into the American national political arena. No longer are the political aspirations of black women restricted to such traditional jobs as ward and precinct leaders or advisers to elected officials. In 1976 there were four duly elected black congresswomen: Shirley Chisholm of New York, Barbara Jordan of Texas, Yvonne Braithwaite Burke of California, and Cardiss Collins of Illinois. They comprised 25 percent of the female delegation in the House of Representatives. It is hoped that the future careers of these black women will not be limited solely to the House of Representatives. Both Representative Chisholm's campaign for the Democratic party presidential nomination in 1972 and Representative Jordan's performance during the 1974 House Judiciary Committee's impeachment proceedings against former president Richard M. Nixon are signs of the expanded political role of black women. But Shirley Chisholm's "good fight" was not the first waged by a black woman in pursuit of either of the nation's two highest elective offices. That distinction belongs to Charlotta A. Bass, the former editor and publisher of the *California Eagle* and a long-time fighter for civil rights on the West Coast, who ran as the vice-presidential candidate of the Progressive party in 1952. Because she ran as the nominee of a controversial third party that received far less than 1 percent of the popular vote, her candidacy has generally been dismissed or overlooked by most historians and political scientists alike. A study of the 1948 campaign of the Progressive party nominee Henry Wallace dismissed the 1952 campaign as that of the party's radical fringe. According to Karl Schmidt, the 1952 Progressive party waved a "tattered, shrinking, now crimson-hued banner."

Hanes Walton, a student of black participation in the American political party system, has erroneously stated that in 1952 "all of its [the Progressive party's] Negro supporters had left the party ranks." New Left historian Barton Bernstein, a student of the Truman administration, is one of the few writers to critically examine the 1952 Progressive party campaign. Although conscious of the party's poor showing, Bernstein praises the Progressives as "heirs to a part of the Nation's radical tradition."[1]

But interest in Bass's candidacy should not be generated solely because she was another "Negro first," particularly as a black female office seeker. Rather, her campaign should be viewed with particular interest because many of the issues that she and the presidential candidate, Vincent Hallinan, espoused, especially in the realm of foreign affairs, have become realities in the 1960s and the 1970s. It is the intent of this paper to analyze the vice-presidential campaign waged by Charlotta Bass in 1952.

Although she has been described by one historian as an "unknown," Charlotta A. Bass was long active in the fight for racial equality in the United States. As editor and publisher of the now defunct *California Eagle,* then the oldest black newspaper on the West Coast, she had fought against restrictive covenants in housing and segregated schools in Los Angeles. She had also taken part in successful campaigns to end job discrimination at the Los Angeles General Hospital, the Los Angeles Rapid Transit Company, the Southern California Telephone Company, and the Boulder Dam Project. Bass was present at the 1919 Pan-African Conference in Paris, was copresident of the Los Angeles division of Marcus Garvey's United Negro Improvement Association during the early 1920s, and was a West Coast promoter of the "Don't Buy Where You Can't Work" campaigns of the mid to late 1930s. In addition to her membership in the NAACP and the Council of African Affairs, Bass served in 1952 as the National Chairman of the Sojourners for Truth and Justice, an organization of black women set up to protest racial violence in the South.[2]

Politically, Bass was no novice, although she never held an elective political office. Long active in the Republican party, she was the western regional director of the 1940 presidential campaign of Wendell Willkie. Despite her ties to the Republican party, Bass exhibited streaks of political independence. In 1928, she had supported Al Smith; in 1932 and 1944, she had supported Franklin D. Roosevelt. Her alternating votes in presidential elections should not be viewed as inconsistencies. Bass supported those candidates—Smith in 1928, Roosevelt in 1932 and 1944, and Willkie in 1940—who advocated both domestic reforms and a more enlightened foreign policy.[3]

Her formal break with the Republican party came in late 1947 over

**Charlotta A. Bass**

that party's failure to advocate a strong civil rights program in the upcoming presidential election. Instead of turning to Harry S. Truman and the Democratic party, whom she saw as no better, Bass was one of the founding members of the 1948 Progressive party. Taking an active role in the new party, she was one of the three cochairpersons of "Women for Wallace" and campaigned for the Henry Wallace–Glenn Taylor ticket.[4]

Bass' vice-presidential campaign was not her first attempt to run for an elective position. In 1945, calling for black representation on the Los Angeles City Council, Bass ran unsuccessfully as an independent candidate for council. In 1950, she ran unsuccessfully as the Independent Progressive party nominee for the Fourteenth Congressional District seat previously held by Helen Gahagan Douglas.[5]

The outbreak of the Korean War in 1950 did not weaken Bass's support for the party. Henry Wallace, supporting the United Nations police action in South Korea, left the party. But Bass and other "radicals" within the party saw the war as a blatant example of American neo-imperialism.[6]

As the 1952 presidential elections neared, the fragmented Progressive party geared itself for the campaign. The growing unpopularity of limited war in Korea, charges of Democratic corruption in Washington, and rising taxes and mounting prices seemed, to the Progressives, to provide an opportunity to capture the disenchanted and disgruntled voter. To attract those voters, the party's Candidates Committee unanimously selected Vincent Hallinan, a prominent California attorney who specialized in civil liberties cases, and Charlotta Bass. In announcing their choice of nominees, the Candidates Committee proclaimed:

We offer these candidates as peace candidates. We offer them as new hope to an America sick and tired of the corruption, the militarism, the segregation of and discrimination against the Negro people, and the growing unemployment that has been brought about by both Democrats and Republicans.

It is obvious that the Progressive party, in nominating a white male of Irish descent who specialized in civil liberties cases and a militant sixty-two-year-old black woman sought the votes of ethnic and black Americans, civil libertarians and women. This was particularly evident in the announcement of Bass's nomination. Emphasis was placed on the fact that Bass was the "first woman ever to be named for high national office by any political party."[7]

Nor did Bass ignore the distinction. In her first speech, following her nomination by the Candidates Committee, she stressed both her color and her sex. "I am a Negro woman," she exclaimed. "Some of my people came here before the *Mayflower.*" More important, this speech set the tone for her campaign:

I am more concerned with what is happening to my people in my country than I am in pouring out money to rebuild a decadent Europe or to repress the colonial people in preparation for a new war.

Thus, Bass sought to link events overseas with the domestic status of black Americans. American concern for the welfare of Europe and Asia, she thought, should be secondary to its concern for its black citizens. Furthermore, using an argument common to critics of the Korean War, who feared the coming of World War III, Bass exclaimed "I want no new wars for myself, for my people or for any people."[8]

Meeting in Chicago in early July of 1952, the Progressive party included in its platform several issues that Bass had earlier raised. Emphasizing foreign affairs, the platform called for an immediate end to the war in Korea, "peaceful understanding and peaceful relations" with the Soviet Union, recognition of the People's Republic of China, a neutral Germany, a $50-billion foreign aid program to be handled by the United Nations, and elimination of trade barriers between the United States and Eastern Europe. The domestic program of the Progressive party was more moderate. Basically, it was an extension of the New Deal–Fair Deal, with a much stronger emphasis on civil rights, civil liberties, and women's rights. They supported the Truman proposals for a national housing program, a national health insurance plan, increased spending for schools, and repeal of the Taft-Hartley Act. Going beyond the Fair Deal, the Progressives called for a Fair Employment Practices Commission (FEPC) with effective enforcement powers, federal anti-poll tax and anti-lynching laws, equal job opportunities and job training for minorities, home rule for the District of Columbia, equal pay for women, a minimum wage of $1.25 an hour, and repeal of the Smith, McCarran, and McCarran-Walter acts.[9]

The party unanimously endorsed the candidacy of Vincent Hallinan (then serving a six-month jail sentence for contempt of court) and Charlotta Bass. W. E. B. Du Bois, in supporting the nomination of his long-time acquaintance, stated that "Mrs. Bass represents black America and American womanhood." And, continued Du Bois, "as if one crown of thorns were not enough, she dares wear two." In her acceptance speech, Bass saw herself fit to wear both crowns. Calling her nomination a historical moment for herself, for her "people," and for all women, she expressed great pride in being chosen as a "pioneer" in the fight for peace and freedom. Concentrating on the foreign affairs portion of the platform, she criticized the rearmament of Germany and the continued American support of the oppression of colored peoples. "It is my government that supports the segregation by violence practiced by Malan in South Africa, sends guns to maintain a bloody French rule in Indo-China, gives money to help the Dutch repress Indonesia, props up Churchill's rule in the Middle East and over the colored peoples of Africa and Malaya," she declared.[10] Connecting the overseas military role of the United States with the status of blacks, Bass called for reductions in and reallocations of monies designated for defense. Instead of spending for "death," she advocated a spending for "life" program. The United States government, Bass urged, should create new jobs, raise wages, and build new schools, hospitals, and homes. Furthermore, in accepting the nomination of the Progressive party, Bass attacked the shortcomings of the two major parties:

Can you conceive of the party of Taft and Eisenhower and MacArthur and McCarthy and the big corporations calling a Negro woman to lead the fight in 1952? Can you see the party of Truman, of [Senator] Russell of Georgia, of [Representative] Rankin of Mississippi, of [Governor] Byrnes of South Carolina, or [Secretary of State] Acheson, naming a Negro to lead the fight against enslavement.[11]

In her acceptance speech, Bass had presented a rhetorical, highly emotional indictment of American foreign and domestic policies. Lacking in substance, her acceptance speech had not specifically spelled out how either she or the Progressive party intended to implement her suggestions. Her acceptance speech had presented some of the problems confronting cold war America. It remained for her campaign to provide more concrete solutions.

The initial reactions of the media, white and black, to Bass as the vice-presidential nominee of the Progressive party ranged from outright hostility to guarded praise. *Time,* the publication of conservative Henry R. Luce, briefly mentioned her candidacy. Besides calling the Hallinan-Bass slate "shocking pink," *Time* described the vice-presidential nominee as "dumpy" and "domineering." The magazine accused the party of blowing the "usual blast at U.S. racial discrimination, 'militarism' and 'growing unemployment,'" but not saying a word against the Soviet Union. The *New York Times,* because of the novelty of Bass's nomination, showed an initial interest in the campaign and periodically covered her activities. Black newspapers devoted some news space to Bass's candidacy. (The exception was the *Chicago Defender,* which made no mention of her campaign.) Some, like the *Louisiana Weekly*, proclaimed the nomination of the "first race woman" for the vice-presidency. The *Pittsburgh Courier*, one of the two major black newspapers that later supported Dwight D. Eisenhower, noted the "strong civil rights plank" of the "left-wing" party. Likewise, the *New York Amsterdam News* termed the party as "increasingly more leftist."[12]

A writer for the *Afro-American* called the Bass candidacy a "siren call" for the Progressives. But the most hostile criticism of Bass's candidacy came from her former newspaper, the *Eagle*. Under new leadership, it would later endorse Adlai Stevenson and now denounced the Progressive party as a "stooge" and "stalking horse" for the American Communist party. Bass's candidacy, the *Eagle* argued, was "bait" for black voters. Perhaps remembering the vice-presidential campaign of Communist James W. Ford in the 1930s, the paper envisioned Bass as being used by the party.[13]

Not all blacks were as skeptical of the Progressive party's motives. Professors Lawrence D. Reddick, Clarence A. Bacote, and Robert H. Brisbane of the Atlanta University complex hailed the "gracious gesture" of the Progressives in nominating Bass and described the party's position on civil rights as "commendable." But the three scholars urged blacks to vote Democratic, because a vote for the Progressives would be "thrown away."[14]

The bulk of Bass's support came from the more radical segments in the United States. *Political Affairs*, the monthly publication of the American Communist party, called Bass's candidacy "a shining symbol of the sincerity of that party [the Progressives] with respect to the issue of Negro rights and Negro freedom." The *Daily Worker* saw the Bass campaign as a struggle against racism that typified the "great fight for Negro representation." Bass did enjoy the unqualified support of some blacks. Paul Robeson, praising the party's selection of Bass, said "I shall count it a privilege to vote for her." W. E. B. Du Bois continued to support Bass and urged blacks to vote for the Progressive party slate. Ada B. Jackson of the Congress of American Women called Bass "a symbol of Negro womanhood in the fighting tradition of Sojourner Truth and Harriet Tubman."[15]

Throughout the campaign, Bass's speeches on foreign policy were reflective of her opposition to the American policy of containment. She consistently criticized American involvement in Korea. On one occasion, citing the mounting figures of Americans dead and wounded, then in excess of a hundred thousand, Bass claimed that the war was no "police action" but the possible prelude to a third world war. Like Hallinan, she called for an immediate cease-fire in Korea with negotiations over the issue of prisoners of war to be conducted later by civilian representatives. Although this proposal of the Progressives largely went unnoticed, the *Daily Compass,* a supporter of Stevenson, found the peace offer "clear cut," "interesting," and "profitable." She continued to oppose the rearmament of Germany. Instead, she argued that the money could be used to "rehouse all my people living in the slums of Harlem and Bedford-Stuyvesant." Likewise, she voiced support for the ending of colonialism in Asia and in Africa and called for peace in the Middle East and the survival of Israel. The Jewish state, she thought, should "not be destroyed by blood-and-oil power politics." In addition, Bass saw the People's Republic of China as the legitimate government of the Chinese mainland and called for the recognition of that government and the withdrawal of support of the Chiang Kai-shek regime.[16]

Although the Progressive party's platform stressed the need for a less belligerent foreign policy, Bass concentrated largely on domestic issues and their relation to American foreign policy. Throughout her campaign, she linked the failure of President Truman's civil rights program to cold war hysteria. She repeatedly accused the Truman administration of being "insincere" and doing "nothing" about the "heart and soul" of blacks' problems. Using an argument that has since been repeated by both New Left and revisionist scholars, Bass criticized cold war hysteria in Washington for preventing even "minor gains" for blacks. Truman was severely rebuked for not criticizing discrimination in Washington. Segregation in the capital of the "greatest country in the World," Bass argued, could be abolished if the president "would bring pressure upon the Congress." Making no mention of President Truman's black appointees, numbering over ninety, she termed his appointments of whites, especially to the Supreme Court, as "hurting" the Negro cause. Her anger was particularly directed against Truman's failure to pressure Congress to pass a bill providing for an effective FEPC, Federal anti–poll tax and anti-lynching bills, and a law banning racial segregation in housing.[17]

In addition to criticizing the Truman administration's position on civil rights, Bass called for increased political representation for women and for blacks. She was not advocating more rights for women, but she was acutely aware of the lack of female representation in Congress. To increase the female representation from nine, Bass could offer no solution other than to criticize that paltry number. To increase black representation from two, Representatives Adam Clayton Powell and William Dawson, she called for an end to the poll tax. According to Bass, the poll tax was the "basis for power of Republicans and Democrats in every section of the country."[18]

Like most third party candidates, Bass criticized both major parties and their nominees. The Progressive party, she argued, offered a choice to the American voter in 1952. Seeing no difference between the Republicans and the Democrats, she sarcastically suggested that perhaps the "elephant and donkey have gotten married." Both parties were accused of not discussing the "real" issues in the campaign—peace in Korea, civil rights, and the raising of living standards. Using the classical economic slogan, "Guns or Butter," Bass questioned how either political party could provide for housing, integrated schools, and better medical care when "they are spending all our money and resources in a war on Communism and not in a war on poverty and racism." Bass's solution obviously called for more butter.[19]

Her most biting comments throughout the campaign were directed at the respective presidential and vice-presidential nominees of the two parties. She saw no difference between the candidates and their programs. Whereas one black journalist described both Eisenhower and Stevenson as "extraordinary" men, Bass depicted them as representing "two sides of the same coin—big money." Her bitterest indictment was directed against the "meaningless" civil rights planks espoused by both nominees. She criticized the positions that both men held on FEPC. Stevenson was accused of doubletalk—first opposing and then supporting an enforceable FEPC. Nor was Eisenhower spared from criticism. Citing a statement by the general that fair employment practice legislation could best be handled by the states, Bass remarked that Eisenhower's statement should come as "no surprise." After all, she reasoned, the general had spent his adult years in the "militarist, jim crow atmosphere of the army."[20]

She criticized Stevenson's numerous trips into the South, in which he campaigned for the white southern vote, while Truman campaigned for the northern black vote.[21] She fumed at Stevenson's statement in Richmond, "Many of your [southern] states are among the best governed in the land." In a response to Mary McLeod Bethune, a supporter of Stevenson, Bass argued:

Surely Mrs. Bethune does not commend Stevenson's praise of the Southern "talent for government" by which a white oligarchy keeps itself in power by depriving the Negro of the right to vote. Nor can she join with her candidate in praising as the "best governed states in the land" the states where Jim Crow is King, states which not only tolerate but perpetuate the horrors of the Martinsville Seven, Willie McGee and Harry and Harriet Moore.[22]

Like Bass, the Republicans, in campaigning for black votes, cited the Democrats' "southern strategy." They called the Eisenhower-Nixon slate "a team pledged to fair employment, an end to all segregation and

Jim Crow, and Equality of Opportunity for all." Bass was suspicious of the Republicans' intentions. Running as a "peace and freedom" candidate, she repeatedly criticized Eisenhower's military background and his nebulous stand on civil rights. To Bass, Eisenhower was and always would be "a Texas born General, against FEPC, who favors segregation in the armed forces."[23]

Her attacks against the two candidates for the vice-presidency, Senators John Sparkman of Alabama and Richard Nixon of California, were even more hard-hitting. Bass stated, "I feel I am better than the other two candidates for Vice-President." She viewed the nomination of Sparkman as an "insult" to blacks and challenged him to "speak out against the segregation of my people." Most black Democrats emphasized Sparkman's support of New Deal domestic legislation and hoped that he might become another Harry Truman, another Hugo Black, or another Judge Waties Waring—white men from southern or border states who "grew" in office. Bass was not convinced. Repeatedly, she cited both his record on civil rights: in sixteen years in Congress he had voted against twenty-six civil rights measures, and in 1950 he boasted that he had "always been opposed to civil rights and always will be." Nor had the fact that Sparkman signed a restrictive covenant for his Washington home endeared him to Bass.[24]

To Bass, the junior senator from California appeared to be the personification of all of the evils in cold war America. The Progressive party campaigned on the issues of peace, equality, and free speech. Bass accused Senator Nixon of opposing all three. In one speech, she alluded to her past participation in the Republican party and blatantly commented that she had known the senator since he was a boy and "never knew any good about him." She accused him of consistently collaborating with the Dixiecrats in "sabotaging" any chances for FEPC. Nixon, like Sparkman, had signed a restrictive covenant for his Washington home. The senator from Alabama was an overt segregationist, but the actions of the senator from California were far more reprehensible. But Bass was more horrified by Nixon's red-baiting. Regarding his views on civil liberties, she classified the senator as one of the "concentration camp congressmen." Calling him "one of the chief enemies of the Bill of Rights," Bass held Nixon as one of those "responsible" for the conviction and jailing of the eleven leaders of the American Communist party imprisoned under the Smith Act.[25] Nor did the "Checkers speech"[26] convince Bass of the senator's honesty and integrity. She simply tagged him as "corrupt."[27]

Her attacks did not go completely unnoticed. The Washington edition of the *Pittsburgh Courier* referred to Bass as one of "America's most vigorous and aggressive women leaders." The *Boston Chronicle* described the former editor as a "militant crusader for all minority groups."[28]

Throughout the campaign, Bass stressed the theme "Win or Lose—We Win!" The Progressive party was the party of principle, pledged to "Peace and Equality," not to accumulating the most votes. Therefore, she argued, the party could not "lose" so long as its actions remained consistent with its principles. She reiterated this theme in calling for a large vote for the Progressives in order to pressure the winning party.[29] Two days before the election, Bass wound up her campaign:

Even if we lose the election, the Negro people will fare better in the months and years following the election because the old party politicians will know that we demand action, not promises.[30]

Even a political realist like Bass would have been dismayed by the party's performance in the general election. Out of 61 million votes cast, the Progressives received 140,000—a mere 0.2 percent, which was one-tenth the number of votes received by Henry Wallace in 1948.

How then does one assess Bass's campaign? Politically, the campaign was a failure. But if one examines the campaign from the perspective of a third party, then indeed the Progressives did not "lose." According to historian William Hesseltine, third parties "have performed the function of calling attention to serious problems and pointing a way to their solution." In applying this criterion to the 1952 Progressive party, one can certainly see that the party did call attention to the problems of the cold war and the problems of race.[31] Like her running mate, Bass called for a more enlightened American foreign policy. It would be stretching the point to credit Bass and other Progressives with "détente." But several arguments they raised were later espoused by J. William Fulbright, then chairman of the Senate Foreign Relations Committee, in *The Arrogance of Power*[32] and have since been implemented by American foreign policy makers. Bass, in particular, would not allow either party, especially the Democrats, to become too smug or too nonchalant regarding the black vote. Serving as a gadfly, she helped to keep alive the issue of civil rights in an election campaign viewed by many as a choice between "the lesser of two evils."

The overall significance of Bass's candidacy was symbolic. It was the first time that a black woman had run for the office of vice-president. The symbolic importance was best expressed by a group of Harlem women, who, at the end of Charlotta Bass's campaign said: "Because of you we can all hold our heads a little higher."[33]

# NOTES

## 1. Northern Black Female Workers: Jacksonian Era

1.    Robert Riegel, *Young America* (Westport, Conn.: Greenwood Press, 1949), p. 220.

2.    Walter E. Hugins, *The Reform Impulse, 1825-1850* (New York: Harper and Row, 1972), p. 11.

3.    Elizabeth Cady Stanton, Susan B. Anthony, and Matilda J. Gage, eds., *History of Woman Suffrage, 1848-1861* (New York: Arno Press, 1969), pp. 67-71.

4.    William L. O'Neill, ed., *The Woman Movement: Feminism in the United States and England* (Chicago: Quadrangle Books, 1969), pp. 34, 108.

5.    Riegel, *Young America,* pp. 132-33.

6.    Elizabeth Baker, *Technology and Woman's Work* (New York: Columbia University Press, 1964), p. 10; *Schedules of 1820 Census of Manufactures— Massachusetts,* National Archives, Washington, D.C..

7.    Martin R. Delany, *The Condition, Elevation, Emigration and Destiny of the Colored People of the United States* (Philadelphia: By the author, 1852), p. 94.

8.    *North Star* (Rochester) 20 October 1848, p. 1.

9.    Edward S. Abdy, *Journal of a Residence and Tour in the United States of America, from April 1833, to October 1834,* 2 vols. (London: J. Murray, 1935), 1: 358.

10.    Harriet Martineau, *Society in America* 2 vols. (New York: Saunders & Otley, 1837), 2: 54.

11.    *The Negro Labor Question, By a N-Y Merchant* (New York: John A. Gray, 1858), p. 3.

12.    Hosea Easton, *A Treatise on the Intellectual Character, and Civil and Political Condition of the Colored People of the United States* (Boston: I. Knapp, 1837), p. 43.

13.    Leon Litwack, *North of Slavery: Negro in the Free States, 1790-1860* (Univeristy of Chicago Press, 1961), p. 155.

14.    John E. Cairnes, *The Slave Power: Its Character, Career, and Probable Designs* (New York: Carleton Publishers, 1862), p. 40.

15.    Caroline F. Ware, *The Early New England Cotton Manufacture: A Study of Industrial Beginnings* (Boston: Houghton Mifflin, 1931), p. 202.

119

16.   Henry A. Miles, *Lowell, As It Was, and As It Is* (Lowell: Nathaniel L. Dayton, 1847), p. 144.
17.   Sarah M. Grimké, *Letters on the Equality of the Sexes and the Conditions of Women* (Boston: Isaac Knapp, 1838), p. 53; Litwack, *North of Slavery*, p. viii.
18.   Giles B. Jackson and D. Webster Davis, *The Industrial History of the Negro Race of the United States* (Richmond: The Virginia Press, 1908; reprinted, Freeport, Conn.: Books for Libraries Press, 1971), p. 133.
19.   *The Rights of All* (New York), 29 May 1829, pp. 2-3; "Tyranny of the Spindle," *Human Rights*, February 1837, p. 1.
20.   Douglas T. Miller, *The Birth of Modern America, 1820-1850* (New York: Western Publishing Company, 1970), p. 102.
21.   Grimké, *Letters*, p. 54.
22.   Oscar Handlin, *Boston's Immigrants: A Study in Acculturation* (Cambridge: Harvard University Press, 1959), p. 73.
23.   John Hope Franklin, *From Slavery to Freedom: A History of Negro Americans*, 3d ed. (New York: Vintage Books, 1969), p. 220.
24.   Lorenzo J. Greene and Carter G. Woodson, *The Negro Wage Earner* (New York: AMS Press, 1930), pp. 1-3.
25.   Grimké, *Letters*, p. 51.
26.   *Statistical Inquiry into the Conditions of the People of Colour, of the City and Districts of Philadelphia* (Philadelphia: Kite and Walton, 1849), pp. 17-18.
27.   Roi Ottley and William J. Weatherby, eds., *The Negro in New York: An Informal Social History, 1800-1827* (New York: New York Public Library, 1967), p. 64.
28.   Simeon F. Moss, "Persistence, Slavery and Involuntary Servitude in a Free State, 1685-1866," *Journal of Negro History* 35 (July 1950): 310; *Minutes of the Fourth Annual Convention for Improvement of the Free People of Color in the United States* (New York, 1834), p. 24.
29.   Ira V. Brown, *The Negro in Pennsylvania History* (University Park: Pennsylvania Historical Association, 1970), p. 37; Elleanor Eldridge, *Memoirs* (Providence: B. T. Albro, 1840), p. 67.
30.   Moss, "Persistence, Slavery and Involuntary Servitude," p. 310.
31.   Delany, *Condition, Elevation, Emigration*, p. 47.
32.   Franklin, *From Slavery to Freedom*, p. 325.
33.   Sylvia G. O. Dannett, *Profiles of Negro Womanhood* (New York: M. W. Lads, 1964), 1: 73; *The Rights of All* (New York), 29 May 1829, p. 8.
34.   Eldridge, *Memoirs*, p. 33.
35.   *Colored American* (New York), 11 November 1837, p. 3.
36.   Dannett, *Profiles of Negro Womanhood*, p. 79.
37.   Jackson and Davis, *The Industrial History of the Negro*, p. 133.
38.   Delany, *Condition, Elevation, Emigration*, p. 43.
39.   Ibid., p. 198.
40.   *Freedom's Journal* (New York), 22 June 1827, p. 60.
41.   Delany, *Condition, Elevation, Emigration*, p. 199.
42.   Jackson and Davis, *Industrial History of the Negro*, p. 137.
43.   Delany, *Condition, Elevation, Emigration*, pp. 198, 200.
44.   *Colored American* (New York), 2 June 1838, p. 60.
45.   *The National Anti-Slavery Standard* (New York), 5 June 1845, p. 3.
46.   *Northern Star and Freemen's Advocate* (New York), 7 April 1842, p. 48; 14 April 1842, p. 52.
47.   Ibid., 3 March 1842, p. 26.
48.   "Ladies Beware," *Colored American* (New York), 18 May 1839, p. 3.
49.   *Freedom's Journal* (New York), 6 June 1828.
50.   Ibid., 30 March 1827, p. 11.
51.   Franklin, *From Slavery to Freedom*, p. 234.
52.   *Human Rights* (New York), February 1836, p. 1.

53.   Lee Benson, *The Concept of Jacksonian Democracy: New York as a Test Case* (Princeton University Press, 1961), p. 89.

54.   Edward Pessen, *Jacksonian America: Society, Personality and Politics* (Homewood, Ill.: The Dorsey Press, 1969), p. 66.

## 2. Discrimination against Afro-American Women in the Woman's Movement

1.   For white feminists who encouraged black women, see Susan B. Anthony and Ida Husted Harper, eds., *History of Woman Suffrage, 1883–1900* (New York: Arno Press and the *New York Times,* 1969), pp. 395, 398–99; Josephine St. Pierre Ruffin, "Trust Women," *The Crisis* 10 (August 1915): 188.

2.   Louis Filler, *The Crusade Against Slavery, 1830–1860* (New York: Harper and Row, 1960), p. 179; Eleanor Flexner, *Century of Struggle: The Woman's Rights Movement in the United States* (Cambridge, Mass.: Belknap Press of Harvard University Press, 1959; paperback edition, New York: Atheneum, 1973), pp. 43–44, 89–90; June Sochen, *Herstory: A Woman's View of American History* (New York: Alfred Publishing Co., 1974), pp. 130–34, 390–92.

3.   Flexner, *Century of Struggle,* p. 144; Miriam Schneir, ed., *Feminism: The Essential Historical Writings* (New York: Vintage Books, 1972), p. xiv; Robert L. Allen and Pamela P. Allen, *Reluctant Reformers: Racism and Social Reform Movements in the United States* (Washington, D.C.: Howard University Press, 1974), pp. 145–46, 156.

4.   William C. Nell, *Colored Patriots of the American Revolution* (Boston: Robert F. Wallcut, 1855), p. 351; J. W. Gibson and W. H. Crogman, *Progress of a Race, Or the Remarkable Advancement of the Colored American* (Naperville, Ill.: J. L. Nichols and Co., 1902, 1912), pp. 181–82; Benjamin Quarles, *Black Abolitionists* (New York: Oxford University Press, 1969), pp. 26–30.

5.   Gerda Lerner, ed., *Black Women in White America: A Documentary History* (New York: Pantheon Books, 1972), pp. 362–65; Quarles, *Black Abolitionists,* pp. 48–49.

6.   Filler, *The Crusade against Slavery,* p. 179.

7.   Flexner, *Century of Struggle,* pp. 89–90, 97–98.

8.   Sojourner Truth, *Narrative of Sojourner Truth: A Bondswoman of Olden Time* (Chicago: Thompson Publishing Co., Inc., Ebony Classics, 1970), pp. 102–4, 107–8.

9.   Elizabeth Cady Stanton, Susan B. Anthony, and Matilda J. Gage, eds., *History of Woman Suffrage, 1861–1876* (New York: Arno Press and the *New York Times,* 1969), pp. 310–11.

10.   Stanton, et al., *History of Woman Suffrage, 1861–1876,* p. 849; Elizabeth Cady Stanton, Susan B. Anthony, and Matilda J. Gage, eds., *History of Woman Suffrage, 1876–1885* (New York: Arno Press and the *New York Times,* 1969), pp. 346–47, 358.

11.   Roslyn Cleagle, "The Colored Temperance Movement: 1830–1860" (Washington, D.C.: unpublished M.A. thesis, Department of History, Howard University, 1969), pp. 63, 64–65, 67–69.

12.   Frances W. Harper, "The Woman's Christian Temperance Union and the Colored Woman," *A.M.E. Church Review* 4 (1888): 314.

13.   Frances W. Harper, "National Woman's Christian Temperance Union," *A.M.E. Church Review* 5 (1889): 242–45.

14.   Gibson, *Progress of a Race,* pp. 216–20.

15.   Rayford W. Logan, *The Negro in the United States* (Princeton: Van Nostrand, 1957), p. 52; *Minneapolis Journal,* November 1900, Mary Church Terrell Papers, Manuscript Division, Library of Congress, Washington, D.C.; Anthony, *History of Woman Suffrage,* pp. 358–59.

16.    Ida B. Wells-Barnett, *Crusade for Justice: The Autobiography of Ida B. Wells-Barnett*, ed. Alfreda Duster (University of Chicago Press, 1970), pp. 345, 346–47.
17.    Gibson, *Progress of a Race*, p. 216.
18.    Ibid., p. 226.
19.    Aileen Kraditor, *The Ideas of the Woman Suffrage Movement, 1890–1920* (Garden City, N.Y.: Anchor Books, Doubleday and Co., Inc., 1971), pp. 213–14; Wells-Barnett, *Crusade for Justice*, pp. 229–30.
20.    Ida Husted Harper, ed., *History of Woman Suffrage, 1900–1920* (New York: Arno Press and the *New York Times*, 1969), pp. 55, 59, 60, n. 1.
21.    Kraditor, *Ideas of Woman Suffrage*, pp. 167–68; Walter White to Mary Church Terrell, 14 March 1919, Mary Church Terrell Papers, no. 3.
22.    Anna H. Shaw, "Votes for All," *The Crisis* 15 (November 1917): 19; *The Crisis* 4 (June 1912): 76–77.
23.    Kraditor, *Ideas of Woman Suffrage*, p. 144.
24.    *The Crisis* 17 (June 1919): 103.
25.    *The New York Age*, 10 May 1917, 11 October 1917.
26.    Ida Harper to Mary Church Terrell, 18 March 1919, Mary Church Terrell Papers, no. 3; Carrie C. Catt, "Votes for All," *The Crisis* 15 (November 1917): 20–21.
27.    Filler, *Crusade against Slavery*, p. 179; Quarles, *Black Abolitionists*, p. 179.
28.    Statement of Purpose, Colored Women's Progressive Franchise Association, Biography; D. Bethune Duffie to Hon. I. M. Howard, 29 July 1870, Correspondence, Cary, MAS, 1 September 1874, Mary Ann Shadd Cary Papers, Moorland-Spingarn Research Center, Howard University, Washington, D.C.; Flexner, *Century of Struggle*, pp. 89–90, 97–98.
29.    Stanton, *History of Woman Suffrage, 1876–1885*, p. 828; Anthony, *History of Woman Suffrage, 1883–1900*, p. 922.
30.    See Anthony, *History of Woman Suffrage, 1883–1900;* Anne F. and Andrew M. Scott, *One Half the People: The Fight for Woman Suffrage* (Philadelphia: J. B. Lippincott, 1975); Celestine Ware, *Woman Power* (New York: Tower Public Affairs Books, 1970); Schneir, *Feminism*. For additional sources see a general assessment of the historiography on blacks in the twentieth-century suffrage movement in Rosalyn Terborg-Penn, "The Historical Treatment of the Afro-American in the Woman's Suffrage Movement, 1900–1920: A Bibliographical Essay," *A Current Bibliography on African Affairs* 7 (Summer 1974): 245–59. For a discussion of the stereotyped images of black women, see Mae C. King, "The Politics of Sexual Stereotypes," *Black Scholar* 4 (March-April 1973): 12–23.

### 3. Black Male Perspectives on the Nineteenth-Century Woman

1.    Benjamin Quarles, *Black Abolitionists* (New York: Oxford University Press, 1969), p. 177.
2.    First African Church, *Annals of the First African Church in the United States of America Now Styled the African Episcopal Church of St. Thomas, Philadelphia, by William Douglass* (Philadelphia: King and Baird, 1862), pp. 28–29.
3.    *The Liberator*, 12 December 1845.
4.    Roslyn V. Cleagle, "The Colored Temperance Movement: 1830–1860" (Washington, D.C.: unpublished M.A. thesis, Department of History, Howard University, 1969), pp. 64–65, 67; Quarles, *Black Abolitionists*, p. 178; *The Weekly Anglo-African*, 6 August 1859.
5.    Samuel J. May, *Some Recollections of Our Anti-Slavery Conflict* (Boston: Fields, Osgood and Co., 1869), p. 93; Frederick Douglass, *The Anti-Slavery Movement: A Lecture before the Rochester Ladies Anti-Slavery Society* (Rochester: Lee, Mann and Co., 1855), pp. 28–29.
6.    Quarles, *Black Abolitionists*, pp. 26, 177–79; Benjamin Quarles, "Frederick Douglass and the Woman's Rights Movement," *Journal of Negro History* 25 (January

1940): 35–44; Elizabeth Cady Stanton, Susan B. Anthony, and Matilda J. Gage, eds., *History of Woman Suffrage, 1848–1861* (New York: Arno Press and the *New York Times*, 1969), pp. 506–7.

7.    *The Liberator*, 23 November 1833.

8.    American Moral Reform Society, *The Minutes and Proceedings of the First Annual Meeting of the American Moral Reform Society* (Philadelphia: Merrihew and Gunn, 1837), pp. 42–43.

9.    *North Star*, 5 May 1848; Martin R. Delany, *The Condition, Elevation, Emigration and Destiny of the Colored People of the United States Politically Considered* (Philadelphia: published by the author, 1852), p. 27; Dorothy Sterling, *The Making of An Afro-American: Martin Robison Delany, 1912–1885* (New York: Doubleday, 1953), p. 88.

10.    *North Star*, 7 March 1848; *Douglass' Paper*, 23 December 1853.

11.    James Forten, Jr., *An Address Delivered before the Ladies' Anti-Slavery Society of Philadelphia* (Philadelphia: Merrihew and Gunn, 1836), pp. 1–6.

12.    Quarles, *Black Abolitionists*, pp. 56, 189.

13.    American Moral Reform Society, *Minutes and Proceedings*, p. 24; Robert Purvis, *Remarks on the Life and Character of James Forten, Delivered at Bethel Church, March 30, 1842* (Philadelphia: Merrihew and Thompson, 1842), p. 16; Stanton, et al. *History of Woman Suffrage, 1848–1861*, pp. 376, 688.

14.    Otelia Cromwell, *Lucretia Mott* (Cambridge, Mass.: Harvard University Press, 1958), p. 79; Frederick B. Tolles, ed., *Slavery and "The Woman Question": Lucretia Mott's Diary of Her Visit to Great Britain to Attend the World's Anti-Slavery Convention of 1840* (Haverford, Pa.: Friends Historical Association, 1952), p. 38.

15.    *The Liberator*, 16 October 1840.

16.    *North Star*, 11 August 1848.

17.    Ibid.

18.    Sterling, *The Making of an Afro-American*, pp. 111–12; Victor Ullman, *Martin R. Delany: The Beginning of Black Nationalism* (Boston: Beacon Press, 1971), pp. 163–64.

19.    Sterling, *Making of an Afro-American*, p. 155.

20.    Quarles, "Frederick Douglass," pp. 35–36; *North Star*, 11 August 1848.

21.    *Douglass' Paper*, 25 November 1853.

22.    Quarles, "Frederick Douglass," p. 38.

23.    Elizabeth Cady Stanton, Susan B. Anthony, and Matilda J. Gage, eds., *History of Woman Suffrage, 1861–1876* (New York: Arno Press, 1969), pp. 380–81, 521, 522, 537, 419, 804, 860; Elizabeth Cady Stanton, Susan B. Anthony, and Matilda J. Gage, eds., *History of Woman Suffrage, 1876–1885* (New York: Arno Press, 1969), pp. 61, 63, 74, 128. Note: Charles Remond died in 1873.

24.    Stanton, et al., *History of Woman Suffrage, 1861–1876*, pp. 346–47, 358, 392; Mary Ann Shadd Cary, Speech to Judiciary Committee, Mary Ann Shadd Cary Papers, folder no. 2, Moorland-Spingarn Research Center, Howard University, Washington, D.C.

25.    Stanton et al., *History of Woman Suffrage, 1861–1876*, pp. 382, 390–92.

26.    *Proceedings of the Constitutional Convention of South Carolina held at Charleston, South Carolina, Beginning January 14th and Ending March 17th 1868* (New York: Arno Press and the *New York Times*, 1968), pp. 836–38; Williamson, *After Slavery: The Negro in South Carolina during Reconstruction, 1861–1877* (New York: Norton, 1975), p. 338; Stanton et al., *History of Woman Suffrage, 1876–1885*, p. 828.

27.    Stanton et al., *History of Woman Suffrage, 1861–1876*, p. 540; Stanton et al., *History of Woman Suffrage, 1876–1885*, p. 829.

28.    *New Era* (Washington), 7 July 1870; D. Augustus Straker, *Citizenship, Its Rights and Duties, Woman Suffrage* (Washington: New National Era Printers, 1874), pp. 2, 4, 11–14.

29.    William H. Johnson, *Africans and the Church* (Albany: Catholic Chronicle Press, 1916), pp. 16–19.

124 / NOTES

30.     Alexander Crummell, *The Black Woman of the South: Her Neglects and Her Needs* (Washington, D.C.: published by the author, 1881), pp. 2-3, 7-8.
31.     Monroe A. Majors, *Noted Negro Women: Their Triumphs and Activities* (Chicago: Donohue and Henneberry, 1893), table of contents, v-vi.
32.     Lawson A. Scruggs, *Woman of Distinction* (Raleigh: L. A. Scruggs, 1893), pp. xxii-xv; *The Bee* (Washington), 14 October 1893.
33.     James T. Haley, ed., *Afro-American Encyclopaedia* (Nashville: Haley and Florida, 1895), pp. 118, 129-30, 169, 273.
34.     *The Atchison Blade*, 10 September 1892.
35.     Crummell, *Black Woman of the South*, pp. 5, 7, 12-14.
36.     *The New York Age*, 25 June 1892; *The New York Sun*, 7 August 1895; *The Globe* (New York), 14 January 1899.
37.     Herbert Aptheker, ed., *A Documentary History of the Negro People in the United States: From the Reconstruction Years to the Founding of the NAACP in 1910* (New York: Citadel, 1951, 1968), pp. 679, 687-88.
38.     *The Bee* (Washington), 12 August 1899.
39.     Aptheker, *Documentary History*, pp. 777-78.
40.     Scruggs, *Women of Distinction*, p. iv; *The Globe* (New York), 17 March 1883; Majors, *Noted Negro Women*, pp. vii-ix.
41.     Aptheker, *Documentary History*, pp. 776, 778.
42.     Scruggs, *Women of Distinction*, pp. 34-35.
43.     Editorial, "Our Women," *The Bee* (Washington), 17 March 1894.


## 4. The Black Woman's Struggle for Equality in the South, 1895-1925

1.     Lawson Andrew Scruggs, *Women of Distinction: Remarkable in Works and Invincible in Character* (Raleigh, N.C.: L. A. Scruggs, 1893), p. 14.
2.     Rosetta D. Sprague, "What Role Is the Educated Negro Woman to Play in the Uplifting of Her Race?" in *Twentieth Century Negro Literature: Or, a Cyclopedia of Thought on the Vital Topics Relating to the American Negro*, ed.: D. W. Culp (Toronto: J. L. Nichols and Co., 1902), p. 170.
3.     Rosa Bowser, "What Role Is the Educated Negro Woman to Play in the Uplifting of Her Race?" in *Twentieth Century Negro Literature*, pp. 179, 182.
4.     Sarah Dudley Pettey, "What Role Is the Educated Negro Woman to Play in the Uplifting of Her Race?" in *Twentieth Century Negro Literature*, p. 184.
5.     Mary Church Terrell, "What Role Is the Educated Negro Woman to Play in the Uplifting of Her Race?" in *Twentieth Century Negro Literature*, p. 173; "News Release 1929 from Oberlin College," Mary Church Terrell Papers, Clippings, Moorland-Spingarn Research Center, Howard University, Washington, D.C.; Washington, D.C., Board of Education, Board of Education Minutes, meeting of 26 May 1910, "Special Meeting of the Board of Education," Mary Church Terrell Papers, Moorland-Spingarn Research Center, Howard University, Washington, D.C.
6.     Walter Chivers, comp., "A Report of Results Gained through Cooperative Efforts of College Neighbors," p. 2, Neighborhood Union File, Negro Collection, Atlanta University, Atlanta, Georgia.
7.     "The History of the Neighborhood Union," p. 6, Neighborhood Union File, Box 1, Negro Collection, Atlanta University, Atlanta, Georgia.
8.     "Treating Negro Problem at Basic," *Atlanta Constitution*, February 1911, and "Negroes Inaugurate Educational Movement," *Atlanta Journal*, 12 December 1909, Neighborhood Union File, Box 1; William M. Slaton, Superintendent of Schools, to Mrs. L. B. Hope, 12 June 1912, Neighborhood Union File, Box 1; Katherine Westfall, Corresponding Secretary of the Woman's Baptist Home Mission Society of Chicago, to Mrs. John Hope, 2 February 1916, Neighborhood Union File, Negro Collection, Atlanta University, Atlanta, Georgia; Walter R. Chivers, "Neighborhood Union: An Effort of Community Organization," *Opportunity* 2 (June 1925): 178.

9.  "Report of the Emergency Committee of the Neighborhood Union," 1934, p. 1, Neighborhood Union File, Box 1, Negro Collection, Atlanta University, Atlanta, Georgia.
10.  Chivers, "Neighborhood Union," p. 179.
11.  Petition to the Honorable, The Board of Education at Atlanta, Georgia, 1913; Mrs. L. B. Hope, Chairman in Behalf of the Women's Civic and Social Improvement Committee to the Board of Education of Atlanta, Georgia, 19 August 1913, Neighborhood Union File, Negro Collection, Atlanta University, Atlanta, Georgia.
12.  "Survey of Colored Public Schools, 1913-1914," 1915, Neighborhood Union File, Negro Collection, Atlanta University, Atlanta, Georgia.
13.  Open Letter, Women's Social Improvement Committee to the Editor of the *Constitution,* 3 December 1913, Neighborhood Union File, Negro Collection, Atlanta University, Atlanta, Georgia.
14.  Address to the Committee of the House of Representatives of the City Council, Atlanta, 1915, Neighborhood Union File, Negro Collection, Atlanta University, Atlanta, Georgia.
15.  "The Story of the Gate City Free Kindergarten," p. 1, Gate City Kindergarten File, Box 5, Negro Collection, Atlanta University, Atlanta, Georgia.
16.  Ibid., p. 2.
17.  "The Gate City Free Kindergarten," 1917, p. 4, Gate City Kindergarten File, Box 5, Negro Collection, Atlanta University, Atlanta, Georgia; *Crimson and Gray* 19 (1 January 1929): 5.
18.  W. E. B. Du Bois, *Some Efforts of American Negroes for Their Own Social Betterment, Report of the Third Atlanta Conference* (Atlanta: Atlanta University Press, 1898), p. 57.
19.  Fannie Barrier Williams, "The Club Movement among the Colored Women," *The Voice of the Negro* 1 (March 1904): 101.
20.  A. W. Hunton, "A Social Center at Hampton, Virginia," *The Crisis* 4 (July 1912): 145.
21.  Du Bois, *Efforts for Social Betterment,* p. 117; Sadie I. Daniels, *Women Builders* (Washington, D.C.: Associated Publishers, 1931), p. 49.
22.  The Chautauqua Circle, Minutes of meeting of October 17, 1913–April 21, 1922, The Chautauqua Circle Minute Book I, p. 8, Chautauqua Circle File; Mae M. Yates, comp., Chautauqua Circle Album, 1913-1963, p. 29. Chautauqua Circle File, Negro Collection, Atlanta University, Atlanta, Georgia.
23.  *The Young Women's Christian Association among Colored Women in Cities* (New York: National Board of the YWCA, 1915), p. 1; L. H. Hammond, *Southern Women and Racial Adjustment* (Lynchburg, Virginia: J. P. Bell Co., 1917), p. 14.
24.  *The YWCA,* p. 2.
25.  "YWCA Organizing," 1933, pp. 1, 3, Neighborhood Union File, Box 5, Negro Collection, Atlanta University, Atlanta, Georgia.
26.  Louise Brooks, National Board of YWCA, to Mrs. Hope, 1 March 1917, Neighborhood Union File, Box 5, Negro Collection, Atlanta University, Atlanta, Georgia.
27.  "War Camp Community Service," Mary Church Terrell Papers, File Box 21; "Attitude of Eight Representative Cities of Tennessee, Alabama, Mississippi, and Florida toward Having a Colored Worker Sent Down from Headquarters to Work in the Colored Districts," p. 1, Mary Church Terrell Papers, File Box 21, Library of Congress, Washington, D.C.
28.  N. F. Mossell (Gertrude), *The Work of the Afro-American Woman* (Philadelphia: George S. Ferguson Co., 1908), pp. 31-32; Eleanor Flexner, *Century of Struggle: The Woman's Rights Movement in the United States* (Cambridge: Harvard University Press, 1959), pp. 190-91.
29.  "National Association of Colored Women, Inc., Synopsis Explaining Organization, Activities, Future Trends," p. 1, Mary Church Terrell Papers, Library of Congress, Washington, D.C.; J. L. Nichols and W. H. Crogman, *Progress of a Race: or, The*

*Remarkable Advancement of the American Negro from the Bondage of Slavery, Ignorance, and Poverty to the Freedom of Citizenship, Intelligence, Affluence, Honor, and Trust* (Naperville, Illinois: J. L. Nichols and Co., 1920), p. 178.

30.    Mary M. Carter, "The Educational Activities of the National Educational Association for College Women, 1923–1960" (master's thesis, Howard University, Department of Education, 17 May 1962), pp. 18, 26.

31.    Mary Church Terrell, "What Role," p. 176.

32.    *The Crisis* 4 (September 1912); "Votes for Women," *The Crisis* 10 (August 1915): 178–92; "Suffrage Workers," *The Crisis* 4 (September 1912): 223; Adella Hunt Logan, "Colored Women as Voters," *The Crisis* 4 (September 1912): 242.

33.    Kelly Miller, "The Risk of Woman Suffrage," *The Crisis* 1 (November 1915): 37.

34.    "Background of the Committee on Racial Relations," pp. 16–18, Commission on Inter-racial Cooperation, Collection File No. 17, Negro Collection, Atlanta University, Atlanta, Georgia.

35.    "List of Members of Tuskegee Conference," Committee on Inter-racial Cooperation, Collection No. 17, Negro Collection, Atlanta University, Atlanta, Georgia.

36.    Ibid., p. 13.

37.    Letter, unsigned, to Mrs. Beverly B. Munford, 11 August 1920, Commission on Inter-racial Cooperation, Collection File No. 17; "Report of Findings Committee," Woman's Inter-racial Conference, Memphis: October 6–7, 1920, p. 1, Commission on Inter-racial Cooperation, Collection File No. 17, Negro Collection, Atlanta University, Atlanta, Georgia.

38.    Ibid., pp. 1–3.

39.    Address by Mrs. Booker Washington, Women's Inter-racial Conference, Memphis, Tennessee. Afternoon Session, 7 October 1920, pp. 1–6, Commission on Inter-racial Cooperation, Collection File No. 17, Negro Collection, Atlanta University, Atlanta, Georgia.

40.    Ibid., p. 13.

41.    Ibid., p. 17.

42.    Address by Mrs. Charlotte Hawkins Brown at the Women's Inter-racial Conference, Memphis, Tennessee, Morning Session, 8 October 1920, p. 1, Commission on Inter-racial Cooperation, Collection File No. 17, Negro Collection, Atlanta University, Atlanta, Georgia.

43.    "The Colored Woman's Statement," p. 1, Commission on Inter-racial Cooperation, Collection File No. 17; "Final Statement of the Colored Woman's Statement," p. 6, Commission on Inter-racial Cooperation, Collection File No. 17, Negro Collection, Atlanta University, Atlanta, Georgia.

44.    Committee on Racial Relations, Minutes of Continuation Committee, Meeting of March 29, 1921, p. 7 (typewritten), Commission on Inter-racial Cooperation, Collection File No. 17, Negro Collection, Atlanta University, Atlanta, Georgia: Southern Federation of Colored Women's Club Meetings, June 28–30, 1921, Atlanta, Georgia, p. 2, Commission on Inter-racial Cooperation, Collection File No. 17, Negro Collection, Atlanta University, Atlanta, Georgia.

45.    Charlotte Hawkins Brown, "Negro Women and Race Relations," Women and Their Organizations, submitted by Mrs. Luke Johnson (Atlanta: 7 October 1921), pp. 11, 15–17, Atlanta University, Commission on Inter-racial Cooperation, Collection File No. 17, Negro Collection, Atlanta University, Atlanta, Georgia.

## 5. Black Women in the Blues Tradition

1.    Derrick Stewart-Baxter's *Ma Rainey and the Classic Blues Singers* (New York: Stein and Day, 1970) is one source which attempts to reveal something of these

women as people, not just entertainers. Other than that the only significant writings are biographies of Bessie Smith by Chris Albertson and Paul Oliver.

2. Paul Oliver discusses several female singers in *The Story of the Blues* (New York: Chilton Press, 1969), pp. 58–72, and *The Meaning of the Blues* (New York: Collier Books, 1963). He and Samuel Charters use their books on the poetry of the blues as a basis for describing certain female singers not to illuminate them as a special category but to give examples of certain lyric passages.

3. The origin of the term *classic* is unclear. However, this era saw the shift from blues as a purely improvisational art to a composed form with planned instrumental accompaniment.

4. Eileen Southern, *Music of Black Americans* (New York: W. W. Norton, 1972), pp. 257, 259, 261, and 359.

5. The Storyville area was the tenderloin district, where bordellos and gambling places were openly frequented by well-to-do "gentlemen" of the south.

6. Oliver, *Story*, p. 63.

7. Stewart-Baxter, *Ma Rainey*, p. 12.

8. George Mitchell, *Blow My Blues Away* (Baton Rouge: Louisiana State University Press, 1971), p. 59–68.

9. Oliver, *Story*, pp. 60–61.

10. Stewart-Baxter, *Ma Rainey*, pp. 56–58.

11. William Broonzy and Yannick Bruynoghe, *Big Bill Blues* (New York: Oak Publications, 1964), p. 23.

12. Samuel Charters, *Poetry of the Blues* (New York: Oak Publications, 1963), pp. 38, 73, and 80.

13. Oliver, *Meaning*, index.

14. Charters, *Poetry;* Oliver, *Story;* Bruce Cook, *Listen to the Blues* (New York: Scribner's Sons).

15. Cook, *Listen*, p. 190.

16. Arnold Shaw, *The World of Soul* (New York: Cowles Book Comapny, 1970), p. 44.

17. Paul Oliver, *Bessie Smith* (London: Cassell Ltd., 1959), p. 3.

18. Oliver, *Story*, p. 64.

19. Cook, *Listen*, pp. 160 and 207.

20. A. X. Nicholas, *Woke Up This Morning* (New York: Bantam Books, 1973), p. 39.

21. In the biography *Bessie Smith*, p. 3, Paul Oliver cites Ma Rainey's marriage at the age of 15; in his book *Story of the Blues*, he says age 17.

22. Oliver, *Story*, p. 61; Stewart-Baxter, *Ma Rainey*, p. 36.

23. Oliver, *Story*, p. 63.

24. Charters, *Poetry*, pp. 46–47.

25. Oliver, *Story*, p. 64.

26. Cited in Stewart-Baxter, *Ma Rainey*, p. 42.

27. Sterling Brown, *Southern Road* (New York: Harcourt, Brace, 1932), pp. 62–63.

28. Stewart-Baxter, *Ma Rainey*, p. 44.

29. Richard Hadlock, *Jazz Masters of the Twenties* (New York: Macmillan, 1965), p. 222.

30. Stewart-Baxter, *Ma Rainey*, pp. 44, 69-70.

31. Sippie Wallace, a private interview in her Detroit home, January 24, 1975.

32. Stewart-Baxter, *Ma Rainey*, pp. 69–70.

33. Oliver, *Meaning of the Blues*, p. 95.

34. Ms. Wallace discussed the text of "Caledonia" in her January 24, 1975, interview.

35. Bonnie Raitt is a young white blues singer who sometimes features the old-time blues artists on her concert tours.

36. Oliver, *Story*, pp. 109–10.
37. Oliver, *Meaning*, p. 78.
38. Broonzy and Bruynoghe, *Big Bill Blues*, pp. 106–7.
39. Cook, *Listen*, p. 122.
40. Oliver, *Meaning*, pp. 35–66, 72, 107, 143.
41. Oliver, *Story*, pp. 90, 110–11.
42. Oliver, *Meaning*, p. 100.
43. Charters, *Poetry*, p. 82.
44. Nicholas, *Morning*, p. 22.
45. Ibid.
46. Shaw, *World*, p. 42.
47. Jack Buerkle and Danny Barker, *Bourbon Street Black* (New York: Oxford University Press, 1973), pp. 37–39.
48. Ms. Olivia Charlot, telephone interview, October 2, 1974.
49. Edith Wilson, personal letter, August 1974.
50. Stewart-Baxter, *Ma Rainey*, p. 31.
51. Helen Humes, private interview during her March 1975 appearance at "The Cookery," a New York supper club.
52. Archie Shepp, renowned jazz artist, lecture, University of Maryland, Baltimore County, March 18, 1974.
53. Mitchell, *Blow*, p. 59.
54. Nicholas, *Morning*, pp. 5–6.
55. Ibid.

## 6. Images of Black Women in Afro-American Poetry

1. Don L. Lee, *We Walk the Way of the New World* (Detroit: Broadside, 1970), p. 39.
2. Paul Laurence Dunbar, *The Complete Poems* (New York: Dodd, Mead, 1913), p. 214.
3. Wilfred Cartey, *Whispers from a Continent* (New York: Vintage, 1969), pp. 3–4.
4. Ibid., p. 38.
5. Gwendolyn Brooks, *The World of Gwendolyn Brooks* (New York: Random House, 1971), p. 377.
6. Ibid., p. 329.
7. Betty Gates, "Mamma Settles the Dropout Problem," *Understanding the New Black Poetry* (New York: William Morrow, 1973), p. 309.
8. Lucille Clifton, "Admonitions," *The Black Poets* (New York: Bantam, 1971), p. 251.
9. Brooks, p. 381.
10. LeRoi Jones, *Blues People,* (New York: William Morrow, 1963), p. 41.
11. Lee, p. 5.
12. Claude McKay, "The Harlem Dancer," *The Book of American Negro Poetry* (New York: Harcourt, Brace & World, 1959), p. 170.
13. Sterling Brown, "Ma Rainey," *Southern Road* (Boston: Beacon, 1974), pp. 63–64.
14. Nikki Giovanni, "Poem for Aretha," *Black Poets,* p. 329.
15. Robert Hayden, ed., *Kaleidoscope* (New York: Harcourt, Brace & World, 1967), p. xx.
16. John Wesley Holloway, "Miss Melerlee," *Book of American Negro Poetry,* pp. 134–35.
17. Gwendolyn Bennett, "To a Dark Girl," *Book of American Negro Poetry,* p. 243.

18. Langston Hughes, "When Sue Wears Red," *Understanding the New Black Poetry*, p. 126.
19. Brooks, p. 37.
20. Ibid., p. 14.
21. Ibid., p. 88.
22. Ibid., p. 45.
23. Ishmael Reed, "To a Daughter of Isaiah," *Chattanooga* (New York: Random House, 1972), p. 35.
24. Michael Harper, "Echoes: One," *Dear John, Dear Coltrane* (University of Pittsburgh Press, 1970), p. 24.
25. Ibid., p. 69.
26. Brooks, p. 324.
27. Ibid., p. 377.
28. Dougherty Long, "Ginger Bread Mamma," *Black Poets*, p. 310.
29. Lucille Clifton, "If I Stand in My Window," *Black Poets*, p. 251.
30. Carolyn Rodgers, "Me, in Kulu Se & Karma," *Understanding the New Black Poetry*, p. 345.
31. Dudley Randall, "Blackberry Sweet," *The New Black Poetry* (New York: International Publishers, 1969), p. 103.
32. Everett Hoagland, "The Anti-Semanticist," *Black Poets*, pp. 314–15.
33. Ibid., p. 312.
34. Georgia Douglas Johnson, *The Heart of a Woman* (Freeport, N.Y.: Books for Libraries Press, 1971), p. xx.
35. Georgia Douglas Johnson, *Bronze* (Boston: B. J. Brimmer, 1922), p. 7.
36. June Jordan, *Some Changes* (New York: E. P. Dutton, 1971), p. ix.
37. Mary Ellmann, *Thinking about Women* (New York: Harcourt, Brace & World, 1968), p. 55.
38. Brooks, p. 324.
39. Don L. Lee, "blackwoman:" *Don't Cry, Scream* (Detroit: Broadside, 1969), p. 51.
40. Kay Lindsey, "Poem," *The Black Woman* (New York: New American Library, 1970), p. 17.
41. Ellmann, p. 102.
42. Margaret Walker, "Molly Means," *Book of Negro Folklore* (New York: Dodd, Mead, 1958), p. 545.
43. W. C. Handy, "St. Louis Blues," *The Negro Caravan* (New York: Arno, 1969), p. 473.
44. Mary Helen Washington, "Black Women Image Makers," *Black World*, 23 (August, 1974): 10.
45. Ibid., p. 11.
46. Ibid., p. 13.
47. Larry Neal, "For Our Women," *Black Fire* (New York: William Morrow, 1968), p. 311.
48. Sonia Sanchez, *We a BaddDDD People* (Detroit: Broadside, 1970), p. 6.
49. Mari Evans, *I Am a Black Woman* (New York: William Morrow, 1970), p. 12.
50. Imamu Amiri Baraka, "leroy," *Black Poets*, pp. 215–16.
51. Mari Evans, ". . . And the Old Women Gathered (The Gospel Singers)," *New Negro Poets: U.S.A.* (Bloomington: University of Indiana Press, 1964), p. 79.
52. Robert Hayden, "Runagate, Runagate," *Understanding the New Black Poetry*, pp. 158–9.
53. Ralph Ellison, *Shadow and Act* (New York: Vintage, 1972), p. 94.

## 7. Anna J. Cooper: A Voice for Black Women

1. Biographical Data File, Anna J. Cooper Papers, Box no. 1, Manuscript Division, Moorland-Spingarn Research Center, Howard University, Washington, D.C. (hereafter cited as Anna J. Cooper Papers.)

2.   *Washington Diocese* (clipping), February 1952, Vertical File, Anna J. Cooper, Washingtoniana Collection, Martin Luther King Public Library, Washington, D.C.
3.   Zita E. Dyson, "Biographical Sketch of Anna J. Cooper," *The Parent-Teacher Journal* (May–June 1930): 12.
4.   Letters from Leonard Garver to Anna J. Cooper, 1884, Anna J. Cooper Papers.
5.   Alexander Crummell, *The Black Woman of the South: Her Neglects and Her Needs* (Washington, D.C.: B. S. Adams, 1883), p. 3.
6.   Anna J. Cooper, *A Voice from the South: By a Black Woman of the South* (Xenia: Ohio: The Aldine Printing House, 1892), p. 3.
7.   Ibid., p. 2.
8.   Anna J. Cooper, "The Higher Education of Women," *Southland* 2 (April 1891): 190–94.
9.   Ibid., p. 199.
10.   Cooper, *Voice from the South*, p. 9.
11.   Ibid., p. 29.
12.   Cooper, "Higher Education of Women," p. 190.
13.   Cooper, *Voice from the South*, p. 139.
14.   Anna J. Cooper, *The Life and Writings of the Grimké Family* (Washington, D.C.: By the author, 1951), p. v.
15.   Cooper, *Voice from the South*, p. 96.
16.   Ibid., p. 192.
17.   Anna J. Cooper, "Angry Saxons and Negro Education," *Crisis* (May 1938), p. 148.
18.   Biographical Data File, Anna J. Cooper Papers.
19.   Hollis Lynch, *Black Urban Condition: A Documentary History, 1866–1917* (New York: Thomas Y. Crowell, 1973), p. 234.
20.   Biographical Data File, Anna J. Cooper Papers.
21.   *Who's Who in Colored America*, 5th ed., 1940, p. 134.
22.   The Record (clipping), 1905, Anna J. Cooper Papers.
23.   *Who's Who in Colored America*, p. 134; Anna J. Cooper, "The Humour of Teaching," *Crisis* (5 November 1930), p. 387.
24.   Interview with Regia Bronson (Cooper's niece), Washington, D.C., 10 November 1974; *New York Times* (clipping) 17 January 1907, Mary Church Terrell Papers, Manuscript Division, Library of Congress, Washington, D.C.
25.   Letter from Anna J. Cooper, 1 May 1909, *Class Letters of 1884*, vol. 5, Oberlin College, Oberlin, Ohio.
26.   Biographical Data File, Anna J. Cooper Papers.
27.   Ibid.
28.   Mrs. N. Stone Scott to Mrs. Calvin Coolidge, 1 November 1924, Anna J. Cooper Papers.
29.   Anna J. Cooper to Daisy M. Carter (n.d.), Anna J. Cooper Papers.
30.   *Who's Who in Colored America*, p. 134.
31.   "The Ethics of the Negro" (paper), September 1902, Anna J. Cooper Papers.
32.   Biographical Data File, Anna J. Cooper Papers.
33.   Anna J. Cooper to W. E. B. Du Bois (31 December 1929), in *The Correspondence of W. E. B. Du Bois*, ed. Herbert Aptheker (Boston: University of Massachusetts Press, 1973), p. 411.
34.   Anna J. Cooper, *The Third Step* (autobiographical) (Washington, D.C.: By the author), p. 5.
35.   Biographical Data File, Anna J. Cooper Papers.
36.   Cooper, *Third Step*, pp. 40–41.
37.   *Washington Post*, 10 August 1958, Vertical Files, Anna J. Cooper, Moorland-Spingarn Research Center, Howard University, Washington, D.C.
38.   *The Sunday Star* (n.d.), Vertical Files, Anna J. Cooper, Moorland-Spingarn Research Center, Howard University, Washington, D.C.

39. Constance Green, *The Secret City: A History of Race Relations in the Nation's Capital* (Princeton: Princeton University Press, 1967), p. 224.
40. *The Afro-American*, March 1934, Vertical File, Anna J. Cooper, Moorland-Spingarn Research Center, Howard University, Washington, D.C.
41. Letter from Charles Weller, (n.d.), Anna J. Cooper Papers.
42. *Washington Post*, 10 August 1958, Vertical File, Anna J. Cooper, Moorland-Spingarn Research Center, Howard University, Washington, D.C.
43. Cooper, "Higher Education of Women," p. 192.
44. *Evening Star* (n.d.), Vertical File, Anna J. Cooper, Moorland-Spingarn Research Center, Howard University, Washington, D.C.

## 8. Nannie Burroughs and the Education of Black Women

1. For the year 1910 the Commissioners of Education reported that there were only 141 public high schools for blacks in all of the United States. See W. E. Burghardt Du Bois, *The Common School and the Negro American*. Sixteenth Annual Conference of the Negro Problems held at Atlanta University, 30 May 1911 (Atlanta: Atlanta University Press, 1911), pp. 134–35.
2. National Baptist Convention, *Journal of the Twentieth Annual Session of the National Baptist Convention, Held in Richmond, Va. September 12-17, 1900* (Nashville, Tenn.: National Baptist Publishing Board, 1900), pp. 64, 195.
3. Idem, *Journal of the Twenty-Fourth Annual Session of the National Baptist Convention and the Fifth Annual Session of the Woman's Convention, Held in Austin, Texas, September 14-19, 1904*, p. 330.
4. Idem, *Journal of the Twenty-Ninth Annual Session of the National Baptist Convention and the Ninth Annual Session of the Woman's Auxiliary Convention, Held in Columbus, Ohio, September 15-20, 1909*, p. 34.
5. Idem, *Seventh Annual Report of the Executive Board and Corresponding Secretary of the Woman's Convention, Auxiliary to the National Baptist Convention, Made at Washington, D.C. September 1907*, p. 62; and Earl L. Harrison, *The Dream and the Dreamer* (Washington, D.C.: Nannie H. Burroughs Literature Foundation, 1956), pp. 35–36; "Nannie Burroughs Claims Baptists and Methodists Fuss as a Regular Habit." No title or date given. Clipping found in the Vertical File, Moorland-Spingarn Research Center, Howard University (hereafter cited as VF, MSRC); "Conference Held at National Training School," *Washington Tribune*, 26 November 1938; also "Highly Specialized Work Is Planned by Training School," *The Evening Star*, 26 February 1939. Both clippings found in the Vertical File, Washingtoniana Division, Martin Luther King Memorial Library, Washington, D.C. (hereafter VF, King Library).
6. Harrison, *Dream*, pp. 54–58; "Baptists May Oust Nannie H. Burroughs," *Chicago Defender*, 9 September 1939, clipping in VF, MSRC; "Miss Nannie H. Burroughs Rises in Defense of Training School," *Washington Tribune*, 20 August 1938, clipping VF, King Library; "Nannie Burroughs' School Wins NBC Support," *Pittsburgh Courier*, 4 October 1947, clipping in VF, King Library.
7. Nannie H. Burroughs, *Making Their Mark* (Washington, D.C.: The National Training School for Women and Girls, n.d.), pp. 3–7.
8. U.S. Department of Labor, *The Negro Woman Worker*, by Jean Collier Brown, Bulletin No. 165 (Washington, D.C.: Government Printing Office, 1938), p. 2; Mary Anderson, "The Plight of Negro Domestic Labor," *The Journal of Negro Education* 5 (January 1930): 66.
9. U.S. Department of Labor, *The Negro Woman Worker*, p. 14; Elizabeth Ross Haynes, "Negroes in Domestic Service in the United States," *Journal of Negro History* 8 (October 1923): 395, 414.
10. Burroughs to Archibald Grimké, 14 May 1920, Archibald H. Grimké Papers, box 30, Moorland-Spingarn Research Center, Howard University (hereafter Grimké papers, MSRC).

11.   Haynes, "Negroes in Domestic Service," p. 396.

12.   Burroughs, "Ten Reasons Why We Should Have a Trade School for Negro Girls," Grimké Papers, Box 21, MSRC.

13.   Sadie I. Daniel, *Women Builders* (Washington, D.C.: Associated Publishers, 1969), pp. 123, 128–29.

14.   Mary Talbert to co-worker, 7 April 1919, Mary Church Terrell Papers, Box 3, Library of Congress.

15.   See letterhead on stationery, e.g., Burroughs to Mrs. Booker T. Washington, 18 November 1922, Mary Church Terrell Collection, box 2, MSRC.

16.   *Opportunity*, 2 (December 1924): 383.

17.   National Baptist Convention, *Thirtieth Annual Report of the Woman's Convention, Auxiliary to the National Baptist Convention, Held in Chicago, Ill., August 14-25, 1930*, p. 16.

18.   Burroughs in *The Louisiana Weekly*, 23 December 1933, quoted in Lerner, *Black Women*, p. 553.

19.   National Baptist Convention, *Proceedings of the Fifty-Third Annual Session of the National Baptist Convention, Memphis, Tenn., September 7-10, 1933, and Proceedings of the Thirty-Third Annual Session of the Woman's Convention, Memphis, Tenn., September 6-10, 1933*, pp. 383–84.

20.   Burroughs, "Black Women and Reform," *The Crisis* 10 (August 1915): 187.

21.   Document entitled "International Council of Women of the Darker Races of the World," pp. 1-4, Mary Church Terrell Papers, box 4, LC; Janie Porter Barrett to Mrs. Booker T. Washington, 23 October 1924 and 12 February 1925, Mary Church Terrell Collection, box 2, MSRC.

22.   Document entitled "Washington, D.C.," representing minutes from the Third Annual Meeting of the International Council of Women of the Darker Races, 5-7 August 1923, and listing officers, resolutions and recommendations, p. 2, Mary Church Terrell Papers, box 4, LC; Adelaid Casely-Hayford to Mary Church Terrell, February 1924, Mary Church Terrell Papers, box 4, LC.

23.   "Washington, D.C.," Minutes of the 5-7 August 1923 Conference, p. 1; also Mrs. H. R. McCrorey, Corresponding Secretary of the Johnson C. Smith University to Mary Church Terrell, 14 August 1923, Mary Church Terrell Papers, box 4, LC.

24.   Mrs. Booker T. Washington to Mary Church Terrell, 20 September 1922, Mary Church Terrell Papers, box 4, LC.

25.   "International Council of Women of the Darker Races," p. 3. Mary Church Terrell Papers, box 4, LC.

26.   "Proceedings of the Annual Meeting of the Association for the Study of Negro Life and History, Inc., Held in Pittsburgh, October 24, 25, 26, 1927," *Journal of Negro History* 13 (January 1928): 6.

27.   "Proceedings of the Annual Meeting of the ASNLH Held in Washington, D.C. October 27-31, 1929"; ibid., 15 (January 1930): 4.

28.   Floyd Calvin, "That's Nannie Burroughs's Job and She Does It," *Pittsburgh Courier*, 8 June 1929, quoted in Lerner, *Black Women*, p. 133.

29.   Burroughs to Mary Church Terrell, 6 February 1922, Mary Church Papers, Box 4, LC.

30.   Burroughs to "My dear Friend," 21 February 1923, Box 4, Mary Church Terrell Papers, LC; and Burroughs to "My dear Friend," 1 December 1928, Grimké Papers, Box 21, MSRC; William Pickens, *Nannie Burroughs and the School of the Three B's* (New York: 1921), p. 11.

31.   "Training School Drive Nets $1,600," *The Evening Star*, 16 November 1926, clipping, VF, King Library.

32.   National Baptist Convention, *Thirtieth Annual Report of the Woman's Convention*, p. 8.

33.   "The Woman Who Dared," *Washington Tribune*, 10 May 1934, clipping, VF, King Library.

34.    In a 1950 interview, Burroughs, in the dusk of her life, spoke out against intermarriage. See Era Bell Thompson, "Message from a Mahogany Blond," *Negro Digest* 8 (July 1950): 33.
35.    Burroughs, "Black Women and Reform," p. 187.
36.    Idem, "Not Color but Character," *The Voice of the Negro* 1 (July 1904): 277–78.
37.    Idem, "With All Thy Getting," *Southern Workman* 56 (July 1927): 301.
38.    "What the Belgians Did to the Negro," *The Worker* 3 (February 1915): 1.
39.    Ibid., p. 2.
40.    Burroughs, "With All Thy Getting," p. 301.
41.    Lerner, *Black Women*, p. 552.
42.    Burroughs, "Nannie H. Burroughs Says Hound Dogs Are Kicked But Not Bulldogs," *Afro-American*, 17 February 1934, VF, MSRC.
43.    "School Head Applauds District NAACP for Its Persistence," ibid., 29 December 1934, clipping, VF, MSRC.
44.    Lerner, *Black Women*, p. 552.
45.    Burroughs, "Declaration of 1776 Is Cause of Harlem Riot," *Afro-American*, 13 April 1935, quoted ibid., pp. 408, 409.

### 9. The 1952 Vice-Presidential Campaign of Charlotta A. Bass

1.    Karl M. Schmidt, *Henry A. Wallace: Quixotic Crusade 1948* (Syracuse University Press, 1960), pp. 311–12; Hanes Walton, Jr., *The Negro in Third Party Politics* (Philadelphia: Dorrance and Co., 1969), p. 60; Barton J. Bernstein, "The Republicans Return," in *The Coming to Power*, eds., Arthur M. Schlesinger, Jr., Fred L. Israel, and William P. Hansen (New York: Chelsea House, 1971), p. 3256.
2.    Leonard Dinnerstein, "The Progressives and States' Rights Parties of 1948," in *History of U.S. Political Parties*, Vol. 4, ed., Arthur M. Schlesinger, Jr. (New York: Chelsea House, 1973), p. 3328; Bass campaign pamphlet, 1952, Vertical File, Charlotta A. Bass, Schomburg Center for Research in Black Culture, New York, New York; *Los Angeles Herald Dispatch*, 28 April 1960, Vertical File, Charlotta Bass, Moorland-Spingarn Research Center, Founders' Library, Howard University, Washington, D.C.; Theodore G. Vincent, *Black Power and the Garvey Movement* (San Francisco: Ramparts Press, 1972), pp. 56, 130; *Boston Chronicle*, 1 March 1952.
3.    Charlotta A. Bass, *Forty Years: Memoirs from the Pages of a Great Newspaper* (Los Angeles: Charlotta A. Bass, 1960), pp. 174–75.
4.    Curtis D. MacDougall, *Gideon's Army: The Campaign and the Vote* (New York: Marzani and Munsell, 1965), 3: 597.
5.    Bass, *Forty Years*, pp. 132–33; *Los Angeles Herald Dispatch*, 28 April 1960.
6.    Matthew E. Mantell, "Opposition to the Korean War: A Study in American Dissent" (Ph.D. dissertation, New York University, 1973), p. 53.
7.    Progressive party, "Statement of Candidates Committee," 7 March 1952, NAACP Papers, Box 444, Library of Congress, Washington, D.C.
8.    *Daily Worker*, 2 April 1952.
9.    Kirk H. Porter and Donald Bruce Johnson, comps., *National Party Platforms, 1840–1960* (Urbana: University of Illinois Press, 1961), pp. 487–94.
10.    *Daily Worker*, 14 July 1952, Vertical File, Charlotta A. Bass, Schomburg Center for Research in Black Culture, New York, New York; Bass *Forty Years*, p. 145.
11.    Bass, *Forty Years*, p. 149.
12.    *Time*, 17 March 1952, p. 20; *New York Times*, 7 March 1952, 24 March 1952, 14 April 1952, 14 August 1952, 7 September 1952, 28 October 1952; *Louisiana Weekly*, no date given, Vertical File, Charlotta A. Bass, Moorland-Spingarn

Research Center, Founders' Library, Howard University, Washington, D.C.; *Pittsburgh Courier*, 19 July 1952; *New York Amsterdam News*, 6 September 1952.

13. *Afro-American* (Washington edition), 7 October 1952; *California Eagle*, 20 June 1952.

14. *Boston Chronicle*, 16 August 1952.

15. *Political Affairs* 31 (August 1952): 8; *Daily Worker*, 23 October 1952; Bass campaign pamphlet; *National Guardian*, 11 September 1952.

16. Porter and Johnson, comps., *National Party Platforms*, pp. 490–91; *Daily Compass*, 8 September 1952; excerpts from a speech by Bass in New York City, no date given, Vertical File, Charlotta A. Bass, Schomburg Center for Research in Black Culture; *Black Dispatch*, 25 October 1952, Vertical File, Charlotta A. Bass, Moorland-Spingarn Research Center.

17. *Daily Worker*, 27 July 1952; *Black Dispatch*, 25 October 1952; *Philadelphia Independent*, 12 July 1952, Vertical File, Charlotta A. Bass, Moorland-Spingarn Research Center; *Pittsburgh Courier*, 21 June 1952.

18. *Black Dispatch*, 25 October 1952; excerpts from a speech by Charlotta A. Bass in New York City, no date given.

19. *Philadelphia Independent*, 12 July 1952; *Daily Worker*, 28 October 1952.

20. *Pittsburgh Courier*, 21 June 1952, 9 August 1952; *Daily Compass*, 8 September 1952; *Daily Worker*, 2 November 1952; Bass campaign pamphlet.

21. *Daily Worker*, 26 October 1952.

22. *Daily Compass*, 28 October 1952.

23. "Republican party campaign literature for Negro voters," NAACP Papers, Box 444, Library of Congress, Washington, D.C.; Bass campaign pamphlet.

24. *Standard Star* (New Rochelle, N.Y.), 14 October 1952; *Daily Worker*, 28 September 1952; Bass campaign pamphlet.

25. *Standard Star* (New Rochelle, N.Y.), 14 October 1952; Bass campaign pamphlet; excerpts from a speech by Bass in New York City, no date given; *Daily Worker*, 21 August 1952. Vertical File, Charlotta A. Bass, Schomburg Center for Research in Black Culture.

26. In mid-September 1952, it was reported that a group of wealthy Californians had contributed over $18,000 to a secret fund that paid Richard Nixon's political expenses. Nixon was under heavy pressure from within the Republican party to withdraw from the ticket. However, he decided to prove his innocence to the American people. In a nationally televised speech, Nixon stated that he had done no wrong in accepting money from the fund. The speech was dubbed the "Checkers speech" because of Nixon's mention of Checkers, the family dog, also a gift. The speech was an overwhelming success, and Nixon remained on the ticket.

27. *Daily Worker*, 26 October 1952.

28. *Pittsburgh Courier* (Washington edition), 4 October 1952; *Boston Chronicle*, 1 November 1952.

29. *Daily Worker*, 13 July 1952, 14 September 1952; *Daily Compass*, 28 October 1952.

30. *New York Amsterdam News*, 1 November 1952.

31. William B. Hesseltine, *The Rise and Fall of Third Parties* (Washington, D.C.: Public Affairs Press, 1948), pp. 9–10; Bernstein, "The Republicans Return," p. 3256.

32. J. William Fulbright, *The Arrogance of Power* (New York: Random House, 1966): see chapters 10 and 11.

33. *Daily Worker*, 31 October 1952.

# PHOTO CREDITS

Chapter 1:    **Frances E.W. Harper**
Moorland Spingarn Research Center
Howard University
Washington, DC

Chapter 2:    **Fannie Barrier Williams**
Photographer Collection
Moorland Spingarn Research Center
Howard University
Washington, DC

Chapter 3:    **Robert Purvis**
Sophia Smith Collection
Smith College
Northhampton, MA 01063

Chapter 4    **Charlotte Hawkins Brown**
The Association For The Study of Afro-American
Life And History
Washington, DC

Chapter 5    **Mamie Smith and Her Jazz Hounds**
Manuscripts, Archives, and Rare Books Division
Schomburg Center for Research in Black Culture
The New York Public Library
Astor, Lenox and Tilden Foundations

Chapter 6    **Gwendolyn Brooks**
Photographs and Prints Division
Schomburg Center for Research in Black Culture
The New York Public Library
Astor, Lenox and Tilden Foundations

Chapter 7    **Anna Julia Cooper**
             Moorland Spingarn Research Center
             Howard University
             Washington, DC

Chapter 8    **Nannie Helen Burroughs**
             Moorland Spingarn Research Center
             Howard University
             Washington, DC

Chapter 9    **Charlotta A. Bass**
             Herald Examiner Collection
             Los Angeles Public Library

# INDEX